P9-DNW-475

THE KINGFISHER FIRST ENCYCLOPEDIA OF ANIMALS

DAVID BURNIE AND LINDA GAMLIN

Editors: Stuart Cooper and Kate Scarborough
Designed by: Sandra Begnor, Julian Ewart, Ralph Pitchford

KINGFISHER
a Houghton Mifflin Company imprint
215 Park Avenue South
New York, New York 10003
www.houghtonmifflinbooks.com

First published in hardcover in 1994
First published in paperback in 1999
10 9 8 7 6 5 4 3 2 (HC)
10 9 8 7 6 5 4 3 2 (PB)

2TR/0502/PROSP/HBM(HBM)/128MA

LIBRARY OF CONGRESS CATALOGING-IN-PUBLICATION DATA
Burnie, David.
The Kingfisher first encyclopedia of animals/by David Burnie & Linda Gamlin.
— 1st American ed.
p. cm.
Includes index.
1. Animals—Encyclopedias, Juvenile literature. [1. Animals—Encyclopdias.]
1. Gamlin, Linda. II. Title. III. Title: First encyclopedia of animals.
QL7.B87 1994
591'.03—dc20 93-46611 CIP AC

ISBN 1-85697-994-6 (HC)
ISBN 0-7534-5259-6 (PB)

The publishers wish to thank the following artists for contributing to this book:

Stephen Adams, Graham Allen, Craig Austin, Bob Bampton, T. Boyer, N. Burgis, J. Butler, Jim Channel, Richard Coombes, Joanne Cowne, Wayne Ford, Chris Forsey, John Francis, Ray Grinaway, Alan Harris, David Holmes (Garden Studio), Ian Jackson, Roger Kent, C.J. King, Terence Lambert, Mick Loates (Linden Artists), Andrew MacDonald, Alan Male (Linden Artists), Josephine Martin (Garden Studio), Doreen McGuinness, Brian McIntyre, William Oliver, Denys Ovendon, Bruce Pearson, Justine Peek (Kathy Jakeman Illustration), Clive Pritchard (Linden Artists), Gordon Riley, Steven Roberts (Wildlife Art Agency), Bernard Robinson, Eric Robson, Peter Scott (Wildlife Art Agency), Nick Shewring, Libby Taylor, Myke Taylor (Garden Studio), John Thompson, Kevin Toy, Guy Troughton, T.K. Wayte, Phil Weare, Norman Weaver, David Webb, Ann Winterbotham, David Wright.

Habitat features by:
Joanne Cowne pp. 108/109; Eugene Fleury pp. 62/63; Chris Forsey pp. 34/35, 80/81; Ray Grinaway pp. 32/33; Bernard Long pp. 38/39; Justine Peek pp. 34/35; Bernard Robinson pp. 116/117; Peter Scott pp. 100/101; Guy Troughton pp. 88/89, 130/131.

The publishers would also like to thank Andy Archer, Dawn Davies, Matthew Gore, Bernard Nussbaum, Narinder Sahotay, and Janet Woronkowicz for their invaluable assistance.

THE KINGFISHER FIRST ENCYCLOPEDIA OF ANIMALS

DAVID BURNIE AND LINDA GAMLIN

KINGfISHER
NEW YORK

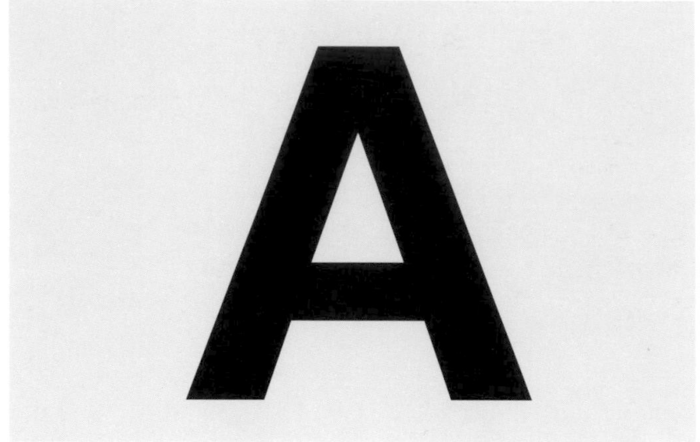

aardvark

The aardvark is one of the world's most unusual kinds of MAMMAL. It lives in Africa, and spends the daytime hidden underground in a large burrow. At night, it comes to the surface to feed on ants and termites. The aardvark finds its food by smell. It is about the size of a pig.

▼ An aardvark rips open ants' nests with its powerful claws, and catches the ants with its sticky tongue.

adder

Adders are fat SNAKES that live in many parts of the world. They can be up to 6 feet (2 m) long, and most of them are very poisonous. When an adder attacks, it bites with special hollow teeth called fangs. The fangs inject a powerful poison. The adder then waits until its food is dead, and swallows it whole.

African wild dog

With their long legs, big ears, and blotchy fur, African wild dogs look quite different to the dogs we keep as pets. They live on the plains of tropical Africa, and they survive by hunting in large groups called packs. When darkness falls, they set off to find food. Although each dog is quite small, together they can kill an animal as big as a zebra.

albatross

Albatrosses are large seabirds that live in the southern half of the world. They have long, hooked beaks, and they feed by snapping up fish and other animals from the sea's surface. The biggest albatrosses have wings that measure over $11\frac{1}{2}$ feet (3.5 m) from tip to tip, which is longer than the wings of any other bird.

alligator

Alligators are powerful REPTILES that spend all their time in or near water. They live mainly in North and South America. Like their close relatives, the CROCODILES, they live by hunting, and they have strong jaws packed with sharp, pointed teeth. A large alligator can be up to 16 feet (5 m) long. When it is in the water, only its eyes and nostrils can be seen. But if it spots a likely meal, such as a fish, it suddenly

▼ An alligator's body is covered with hard scales. The scales on its back are bony, and work like a suit of armor.

lunges forward by flicking its long and flattened tail, and grabs its prey. On land, alligators move around quite slowly on their short, stubby legs.

American eagle see **bald eagle**

amoeba

The amoeba is a tiny animal that can usually be seen only with a microscope. Its body is made up of one compartment, or cell, and has no fixed shape. When the amoeba moves, it stretches out in one direction, and the rest of its body follows. Amoebas live mainly in water, and feed on other single-celled animals.

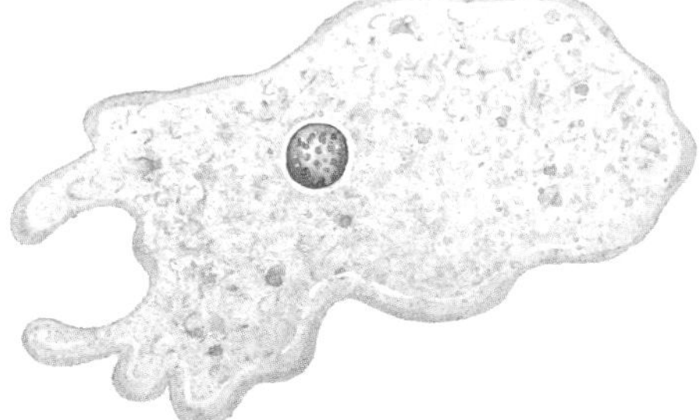

▶ An amoeba is like a tiny bag of jelly. It does not have eyes or a mouth.

amphibians

Amphibians are animals that live partly on land and partly in water. Some spend nearly all their lives in ponds, lakes, or rivers. Others live mainly on land, and return to water only to breed. There are two main groups of amphibians, the FROGS and TOADS, and the NEWTS and SALAMANDERS. Frogs and toads have powerful legs, but no tails. Newts and salamanders have weaker legs, but their tails can be as long as their bodies. All amphibians lay jellylike eggs, either in or near water. When an amphibian's eggs hatch, they produce small swimming animals called tadpoles. As a tadpole grows up, it slowly changes shape until it looks like an adult.

AMPHIBIANS

Amphibians are found all over the world, except in places that are very cold or dry. Most amphibians have four legs and thin skin. Caecilians are burrowing amphibians that have no legs. Their bodies are covered in ring-shaped scales.

anaconda

The anaconda, from South America, is one of the longest kinds of SNAKE. A large one can reach 30 feet (9 m), which is as long as five adult people laid end to end. Anacondas are not poisonous.

angler fish

The angler fish stays mainly on the seabed. It attracts its prey by waving a wormlike lure in front of its mouth. When another fish comes near to look, the angler opens its huge mouth and snaps it up.

animal
The world is full of many kinds of plants and animals. All of them need energy to survive. Animals get their energy by eating food. Some animals eat plants, while others eat animals. The hunters are called predators, and the hunted are called prey. Some animals are active at night, like owls. These animals are called nocturnal. Scientists estimate that there are about 10 million different kinds, or species, of animal on Earth, and there are many still waiting to be discovered.

animal partnerships see **page 9**

ant
Ants are small insects that always live together. Ants build nests by tunneling underground, or by heaping up leaves to make mounds. In each nest there is one ant, called a queen, which lays eggs. See **army ant**, **honeypot ant**.

▼ These leafcutter ants are collecting small pieces of leaf and carrying them to their underground nest. The ants use the leaves to make a kind of compost on which they grow their food.

anteater
Anteaters are mammals that feed almost entirely on ants and termites. They have very long snouts and long sticky tongues, but no teeth. There are four kinds of anteater, and all of them live in South America. See **echidna**.

▲ The giant anteater is over 3 feet (1 m) long and lives on the ground. The other kinds of anteater live in trees.

antelope
Antelopes are mammals that feed on grass and other plants. Some of them live in huge herds on grassy plains, but others hide away in forests. Most antelopes live in Africa. The horns of the males are usually larger than those of the females. See **gazelle**, **gnu**.

ant lion
An ant lion is an insect grub (larva) with powerful jaws. It digs a steep-sided pit in sandy ground, and waits at the bottom, with most of its body buried. If an ant walks past and tumbles in, the ant lion quickly eats it.

ape
Apes are our closest living relatives. Like us, they are primates, and have large brains. Two kinds of apes, gibbons and orangutans, spend most of their lives in trees. Gorillas and chimpanzees spend a lot of their time on the ground.

ANIMAL PARTNERSHIPS

For animals, survival is a difficult business. Some animals help themselves by living in partnership with another kind of animal. From some partnerships, both animals gain. But others are quite one-sided. One animal gains something, while its partner gets little or nothing in return. A FLEA, for example, forms a partnership by living on a much bigger animal. The flea gets food by sucking blood, but the other animal gets nothing in return. Fleas and other animals that form this kind of partnership are called PARASITES. See **cuckoo**, **remora**.

▲ Oxpeckers pick ticks and other pests from the skin of buffalo. The oxpecker gets a meal, and in return the buffalo gets a clean skin.

▶ A hermit crab's shell makes a useful perch for sea anemones. The anemones get more food because the crab carries them around. The crab benefits because the stinging anemones help to keep away its enemies.

▲ Clown fish live among the stinging tentacles of sea anemones. They eat scraps of leftover food, but do not get stung.

▶ Many animals live in groups or herds, so that when some are eating or drinking, others are keeping watch. Through this kind of partnership, they have a better chance of avoiding attack.

A

aphid

Aphids are INSECTS that are not much bigger than a pinhead. They are often green and they have sharp mouth-parts. Aphids feed by piercing a plant's leaves or stems, and drinking the sugary sap. They can breed very quickly and are usually harmful to crops.

arachnids

An arachnid has four pairs of legs, and a body that is divided into two parts. Nearly all arachnids live on land. They include SPIDERS and SCORPIONS, and also smaller animals called mites and ticks. Spiders and scorpions live by hunting other animals, and they have poisonous fangs or stingers. Mites live on the remains of plants or animals.

ARACHNIDS

Arachnids are found in all but the coldest parts of the world. Spiders and scorpions can be seen, but mites and ticks are tiny and some can only be seen under a microscope.

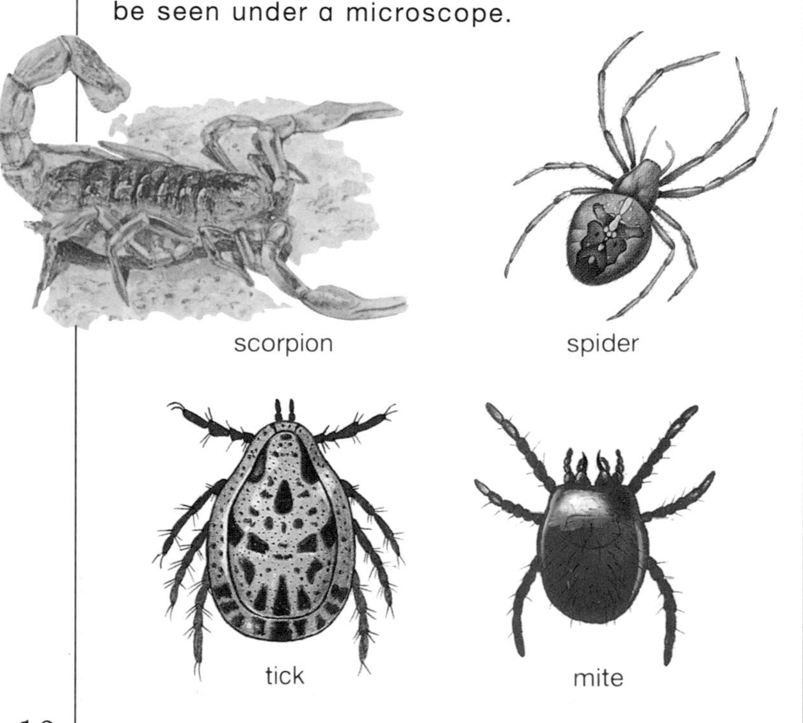

▼ The archer fish is like a living water pistol. It uses a jet of water to bring insects within reach.

archer fish

Many fish feed on insects that fall into water, but the archer fish does not simply wait for food to come its way. If it sees an insect flying above the surface, it squirts a jet of water into the air. The insect tumbles into the water, and the archer fish snaps it up. Archer fish live in Asia.

Arctic tern

Many BIRDS breed in one place, and spend the winter in another. None of them travel as far as the Arctic tern. This small and slender seabird breeds in the far north. Once its chicks can fly properly, it sets off on a journey that takes it all the way to the Antarctic Ocean. Every year the tern flies to the Antarctic and back, covering at least 20,000 miles (32,000 km). As it flies, the Arctic tern feeds by snatching small animals from the water's surface. See **migration**, **tern**.

armadillo

An armadillo is a MAMMAL that is covered by small plates made out of toughened skin. If danger threatens, some kinds of armadillo roll themselves up into a ball, so that the soft parts of their bodies are safely tucked away. Armadillos live in South and Central America.

▲ The nine-banded armadillo rolls up into an armor-plated ball if threatened.

army ant

Most ANTS make nests, but army ants are different. These ferocious insects live in RAIN FORESTS in groups that are sometimes a million strong. The ants spend most of their time on the move. They swarm over the forest floor, killing and eating any animals in their path. As night falls, the ants set up a camp called a bivouac, which is made by ants linking their legs together. When day breaks, the bivouac splits up, and the ants move on.

arrow poison frog

Tiny arrow poison frogs are among the world's most colorful and dangerous AMPHIBIANS. They live in the RAIN FORESTS of South America, and feed mainly on insects. Although they are only about 2 inches (5 cm) long, they have few enemies because their skin produces an extremely powerful poison. Rain forest Indians collect the frogs, and smear the poison onto the tips of their arrows.

arthropods

Arthropods are animals that have a tough case on the outside of their bodies. The case is made of separate plates, and it has special hinges so that the animal can move. INSECTS are arthropods, and so too are CRUSTACEANS, ARACHNIDS, CENTIPEDES, and MILLIPEDES. Scientists know that there are at least one million kinds of arthropod on Earth, and they are sure that many more have yet to be discovered.

ARTHROPODS

An arthropod has a hard body, and legs with hinged joints. On land, the most common arthropods are insects and spiders. Insects are also found in fresh water, but they do not live in the sea. Crustaceans are found in seas throughout the world.

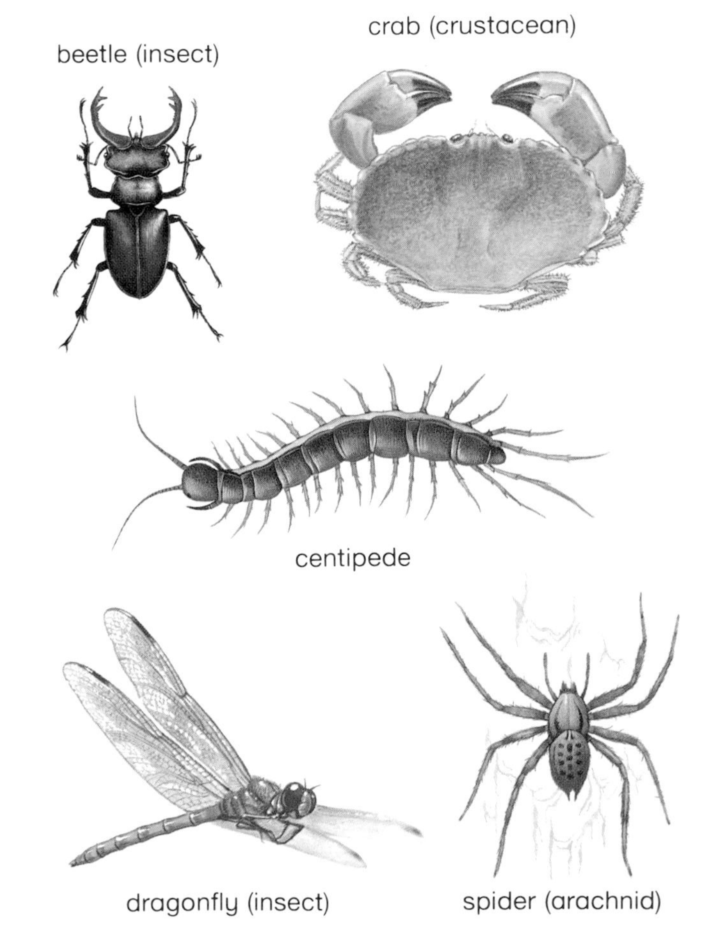

A

◀ An avocet feeds on insects and crustaceans. This is a European avocet.

avocet

If you see a waterbird with long legs and a sharply upturned beak, it is probably an avocet. Avocets live on coasts and in wetlands throughout the world, including Australia. They feed by striding through the water, and swinging their beaks from side to side below the water surface. If they feel a fish or any other small animal, they quickly swallow it.

◀ The aye-aye is one of the world's strangest primates. It has specially long middle fingers, and it uses these to tap on branches. If the tapping disturbs a wood-boring insect, the aye-aye hears it move, and pulls away at the wood to get at its food.

aye-aye

The aye-aye is a PRIMATE that lives in the forests of Madagascar. It is about as big as a cat, and is active only at night. Aye-ayes feed on fruit and insect grubs. They have very long, thin fingers, and they use the longest like a toothpick, to pick grubs from crevices in bark.

baboon

Baboons are powerful MONKEYS that live in Africa. They have strong legs and long muzzles, and spend most of their time on the ground. Baboons live in groups, called troops, which can contain up to 200 animals. The biggest males are in charge of the troop, and they protect the females and young. Baboons have large teeth, and they feed on almost anything, including fruit and leaves.

badger

People do not often see badgers, because they spend the daytime hidden underground. At night, they come to the surface to look for fruit, worms, and other small animals. Badgers are MAMMALS. They live in Europe, Asia, and North America, and can be 3 feet (1 m) long.

▶ A badger has short legs with sharp claws, which it uses for digging its burrow, This is an Old World badger. The American badger is smaller and has less white on its head.

bald eagle

The bald eagle is not really bald but has white feathers on its head that make it appear bald from a distance. It has a wingspan of 8 feet (2.5 m). The bald eagle lives close to water, and its main food is fish, which it grabs from the water with its sharp claws. At one time, bald eagles were widespread in North America, but now they are quite rare. See **birds of prey**, **eagle**.

▶ The bald eagle is the national emblem of the United States.

bandicoot

Bandicoots are MARSUPIALS that live in Australia and New Guinea. They have short legs and a long, pointed snout. Bandicoots are expert diggers. They use their sharp claws to unearth small animals.

bark beetle

Bark beetles are insects that live under the bark of some trees. The most destructive is the elm bark beetle, which carries Dutch elm disease. This disease has killed millions of trees throughout the world.

barn owl

The beautiful barn owl is one of the world's most widespread birds. It lives on every continent except Antarctica, and it feeds at night on mice, voles, and other rodents. The barn owl finds its food by flying slowly above the ground. It has extremely good eyesight and hearing, and its feathers have special fringes that make its flight almost silent. See **owl**.

barnacle

Barnacles look very much like MOLLUSKS, but they are actually very unusual CRUSTACEANS. A barnacle spends its adult life glued to a rock on the lower shore. Its body is protected by hard white plates, and it feeds by collecting tiny particles of food from the water.

barracuda

With a body as long as a person, and needle-sharp teeth, the barracuda is a ferocious predatory FISH. Barracudas live in tropical seas, and they usually hunt on their own. They feed on other fish.

▲ Bats are good fliers but when at rest, they hang upside down.

bat

Bats are the only MAMMALS that actually fly rather than just glide through the air. Small bats hunt insects, and they can find their food in complete darkness. They do this by sending out high-pitched squeaks, and listening for the echoes that bounce back—a system known as echolocation. Bigger bats, such as the FLYING FOX, feed on fruit.

bear

Bears are heavy, powerful mammals that have large heads and flat paws. They live mainly in the Northern Hemisphere, although one kind, called the spectacled bear, lives in South America. Bears spend their time alone or in small family groups. They will eat almost anything, including roots, fruit, and small animals. Some are even expert at catching fish as they swim up rivers. See **hibernation**, **polar bear**.

▶ The black bear is a small bear and a good climber. The tall grizzly bear is very fierce.

beaver

Long before humans learned how to dam rivers, beavers were building dams of their own. Beavers are large rodents that live near water. They have webbed back feet, and their tails are shaped like paddles. Beavers eat the leaves and bark of trees.

bee

Bees are insects that feed on pollen and nectar from flowers. They live throughout the world, wherever flowers grow. Bees have long tongues for drinking nectar. Many bees have stingers, but they are not normally dangerous, because they use their stingers only in an emergency. Some bees fly away as soon as they are fully grown, and spend their lives on their own. Others stay together, and live in large family groups. Honeybees and bumblebees both live like this. See **leafcutting bee**.

▶ Before swallowing a bee or wasp, a bee-eater rubs the insect's body to squeeze out the poison.

bee-eater

Most birds stay away from bees and wasps, but bee-eaters are different. These brightly colored birds use their curved beaks to snap up stinging insects. Bee-eaters live in Africa, Europe, and Asia.

beetle

A beetle is an insect that has two very different pairs of wings. Its hindwings are thin, and they often fold up when not in use. Its forewings are very thick, and they can close up over the hindwings like a case. Beetles are the most varied of all insects. So far, scientists have identified about 400,000 different kinds. See **firefly**, **glowworm**, **ladybug**, **weevil**.

▼ The goliath beetle, which is up to 4 inches (10 cm) long, is the biggest and heaviest flying insect.

BEHAVIOR

If you watch any animal, you will see that it responds to things around it in a particular way. This is called behavior. Animals are born with some patterns of behavior, and these are called instincts. For example, a bird instinctively knows how to react to danger, how to attract a mate, and how to build its nest. But animal behavior does not only depend on instinct. During their lives, many animals also learn kinds of behavior from their relatives. Together, different patterns of behavior help an animal to survive, and to breed. See **defense**, **parental care**.

▶ Herring gull chicks hit the red spot on their parents' beak to get food.

▶ Chimpanzees learn much of their behavior by watching their parents. This baby chimp is watching its mother use a simple tool to find insects. In later life, it will also use tools.

◀ Egrets grow long feathers during the mating season and display these feathers as part of their courtship dance.

▶ Beavers make dams out of mud and branches. They work entirely by instinct, gnawing through trees and moving branches to the right place. In the pool behind the dam they build their home—a mound of branches called a lodge.

B

bird-eating spider

Bird-eating spiders live in the RAIN FORESTS of South America. They have fat bodies and hairy legs. With their legs stretched out fully, they can measure up to 10 inches (25 cm) across. Bird-eating spiders hunt by creeping up trees and across the forest floor. They sometimes eat birds on nests, but their usual food is insects, which they catch after dark. They kill their prey with a poisonous bite. See **tarantula**.

▲ The bird-eating spider has large fangs, but a tiny mouth. It feeds by sucking fluid from the body of its prey.

bird of paradise

Birds of paradise live in the RAIN FORESTS of New Guinea and northern Australia. The females look quite dull, but the males have brilliantly colored feathers that are often beautifully shaped. A male bird of paradise uses his bright colors to attract a mate. He perches on a low branch, and then spreads out his wings in an eye-catching display. Usually, the female makes the nest and raises the young.

birds

Birds are the biggest and most powerful fliers in the animal world. There are over 9,000 different kinds of bird, and they live on every continent, including Antarctica. They evolved from the REPTILES and, like them, they lay eggs with shells. Birds are the only animals that have feathers. They use their feathers to fly, and to make their bodies streamlined, and also to keep themselves warm. Birds do not have any teeth. Instead, their jaws form a long beak that has hard edges. Most birds can fly, but some spend all their lives on the ground. Flightless birds include the OSTRICH, which is the largest bird of all.

BIRDS

Birds live in many different habitats, from deserts to the open sea. They vary greatly in size and shape, but they all have feathers.

birds of prey

Birds of prey are hunters. They have eyes that face forward, and strong hooked beaks. They swoop down on their food and grab it with their sharp claws, or talons, and they use their beaks to tear up their food before swallowing it. There are many different kinds of birds of prey, and they live all over the world. The largest are the EAGLES, whose wings can measure over 8 feet (2.5 m) from tip to tip. The smallest are tiny pygmy falcons, which are about the size of a starling. See **falcon, hawk, kite**.

▲ The largest birdwing butterflies have wings that measure 11 inches (28 cm) from tip to tip.

birdwing butterfly

Birdwings are the largest butterflies in the world. They have long, pointed wings, and they flap them quite slowly, just like some birds. Birdwings live in the tropical forests of Southeast Asia and Australia. See **butterflies and moths**.

bison

Bison, which are known in North America as buffalo, are large hoofed MAMMALS that feed on grass. The males have shaggy manes that cover their heads, backs, and front legs, and they can be taller than a person. The females are smaller. See **buffalo, ruminant**.

▼ The African fish eagle snatches up fish with its sharp talons. It spends a lot of time on a favorite perch watching for the movement of fish in the water.

black widow spider

Black widows are small SPIDERS that have a very poisonous bite. They often live in or near houses, and they catch insects by spinning webs. Black widows usually do no harm to humans. However, if someone comes very close, a black widow may bite, and the person quickly becomes ill. Black widows live in many parts of the world. They are most common in warm places such as the southern United States.

blue whale

The blue whale is the largest animal that exists. A fully grown female can be over 100 feet (30 m) long. Blue whales grow to this huge size on a diet of tiny animals called krill. As they swim along, they suck in seawater through their mouths, and then squeeze it through a screen of special fibers called baleen plates. The baleen traps the krill, and the whale swallows them. Blue whales live in all the world's oceans, but they feed mainly in the cold water around the Poles. See **whale**.

◀ Like all snakes, boas cannot chew their food. Instead, they swallow it whole. The boa's jaws can stretch wide apart, so that it can swallow an animal that is much wider than its head. A large meal will last it for several weeks.

boa constrictor

After the ANACONDA, the boa constrictor is the largest SNAKE in Central and South America. Large specimens can be over 16 feet (5 m) long. Boas feed mainly on warm-blooded animals, including birds and mammals. They are not poisonous, and once they have caught their prey, they coil around it squeezing tightly until it suffocates.

bobcat

The bobcat is a wildcat that lives in North America. It is about a yard (1 m) long, and has a spotted coat, and a short stumpy tail. Bobcats hunt at night, and they feed mainly on birds and rodents. Like pet cats, they creep up on their prey and then pounce.

booby

Boobies are seabirds that live mainly in the tropics. They have long, sharp beaks and their feet are often brightly colored. Like their relatives, the GANNETS, boobies feed by diving into the water with their wings folded back. They often feed in flocks, and if they see a school of fish, they all plunge into the water at the same time. Boobies nest on the ground in groups.

boomslang

The boomslang is an African SNAKE that spends most of its time in trees. It has a long, sticklike body and it hides itself by keeping perfectly still. The boomslang has a very poisonous bite.

bowerbird

Male bowerbirds have a very unusual way of attracting females. They collect hundreds or thousands of small sticks, and use them to make complicated bowers on the forest floor, which they decorate with flowers. Bowerbirds live only in New Guinea and Australia.

bristletail

A bristletail is a tiny INSECT that does not have wings. Bristletails spend their lives on the ground, and they feed on small scraps of plants, and dead insects.

▼ Boobies are good at flying, but clumsy on land.

budgerigar
Budgerigars are small PARROTS. They have short beaks for cracking open seeds. They live wild only in Australia, but are kept as pets all over the world. Wild budgerigars live in big flocks.

buffalo
Buffalo are among the biggest and most dangerous of all MAMMALS. A large bull can be 10 feet (3 m) high at the shoulder, and when it charges, it can crush a car. See **bison**.

bug
A "true" bug is an INSECT with sharp mouthparts that it uses for piercing and sucking. An APHID is a bug, so is a CICADA. The word bug does not cover all insects.

bulbul
Bulbuls are some of the most common garden BIRDS in Africa and warm parts of Asia. They are always busy, and many of them have loud songs. Bulbuls have bright feathers and small beaks.

▲ Some bullfrogs live underground in dry places. They come to the surface when it rains.

bullfrog
Bullfrogs are the largest FROGS. There are several kinds of bullfrog, and they live in many parts of the world. The North American bullfrog can be about 8 inches (20 cm) long, and it eats all kinds of small animals, even birds and snakes.

▲ Wild budgerigars are always green with yellow heads. Like all parrots, they have two toes pointing forward, and two pointing backward.

bumblebee
Bumblebees are furry-bodied BEES that live in cool parts of the world. Like HONEYBEES, bumblebees live together in nests, but their nests are quite small. The nest is started by the queen bee. Her eggs hatch into worker bees that gather food and help to raise more young and new queens. In the fall, new queens fly away, and the nest is abandoned.

▶ A bumblebee has a very long tongue that can reach deep into flowers for sugary nectar.

burnet moth

Burnet moths live mainly in Europe and Asia. They are small, but their bright colors make them easy to see. Burnet moths often fly by day. Their colors warn birds that they contain bad-tasting chemicals. See **butterflies and moths**.

burrowing owl

In the treeless plains of North and South America, the burrowing owl makes its home underground. Burrowing owls are only about the size of a starling, and they have short tails and long legs. They feed mainly on insects. See **owl**.

▼ Burrowing owls stand near the entrance of their burrows, and bob up and down if anything disturbs them.

burying beetle

Burying beetles roam the ground after dark, searching for the dead bodies of small animals such as mice or birds. When they find a body, they bury it, and then lay their eggs in a chamber close by. When the beetle grubs hatch, they feed on the buried body. Some are black, but others have bright orange bands across their backs. See **beetle**.

▲ Bushbabies search for food after dark. They eat many different things, including seeds, insects, and birds' eggs.

bushbaby

A bushbaby is a PRIMATE with big eyes and a long, furry tail. It is an expert climber, and spends nearly all its time in trees. Bushbabies live in the forests of Africa. There are two kinds of bushbaby. One is about the size of a squirrel, and the other is twice as big.

bushbuck

The bushbuck is an ANTELOPE that lives in Africa, south of the Sahara Desert. The sharp horns of the male may reach a length of 2 feet (60 cm). The females may also have horns. The bushbuck is a shy animal and comes out mostly at night. It has, however, been known to kill leopards and wild dogs.

▼ These two burying beetles are covering up the body of a small animal. Burying beetles live in many parts of the world.

bushmaster

The bushmaster is one of the most deadly snakes in Central and South America. It can be over 10 feet (3 m) long, and it hunts mammals at night. A bushmaster has special sense organs that can feel the warmth from a mammal's body. Bushmasters are not common, but they have been known to attack humans.

bustard

Bustards are large birds that live in open grassland. They have long legs and very good eyesight, and feed on seeds and insects. The rare great bustard, of Europe and Asia, weighs up to 44 pounds (20 kg). It is the world's heaviest flying bird.

butterflies and moths

Butterflies and moths are insects that have two pairs of wings, long tongues, and bodies covered by thousands of tiny scales. The scales on their wings overlap like tiles on a roof, and in butterflies they are often brightly colored. There are about 150,000 different butterflies and moths. One of the largest is the Australian hercules moth, which has a wingspan of 11 inches (28 cm).

▼ Butterflies and moths go through four stages of growth to become an adult. From an egg (1), they grow into caterpillars or larva (2), then they become a chrysalis (3) and finally emerge as an adult (4).

▲ This Eurasian buzzard spends much of its time in the air. It often cries out in flight.

buzzard

In the United States the name buzzard is given to birds of prey such as the turkey vulture and the black vulture. These birds have no feathers on their neck and head. In Europe, buzzards are large hawks that are like eagles in their soaring flight.

BUTTERFLIES AND MOTHS

Butterflies usually fly during the daytime, while most moths fly at night. However, burnet moths, for example, fly during the day and are as colorful as many butterflies.

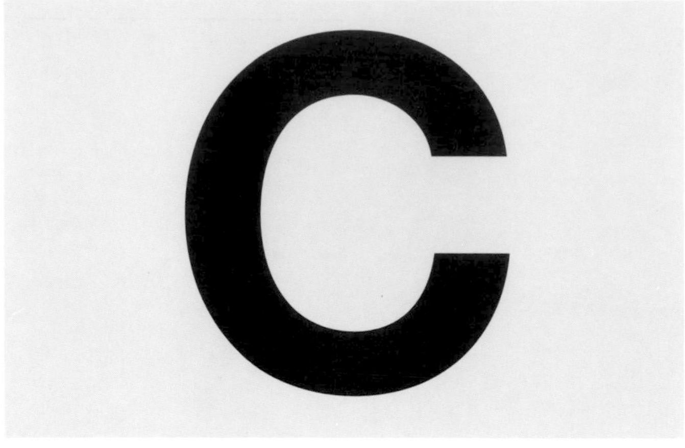

cabbage white

This black and white BUTTERFLY lays its eggs on cabbage plants. Its caterpillars can soon eat their way through the leaves. Cabbage whites often travel to find food. See **migration**.

caddis fly

Caddis flies are brown-winged INSECTS that flutter over streams and ponds in early summer. They spend the first part of their lives as larvae underwater. (A larva is a partly developed adult.)

▼ Many caddis fly larvae fit either tiny stones, or leaves together to make tube-shaped cases. These cases are for protection.

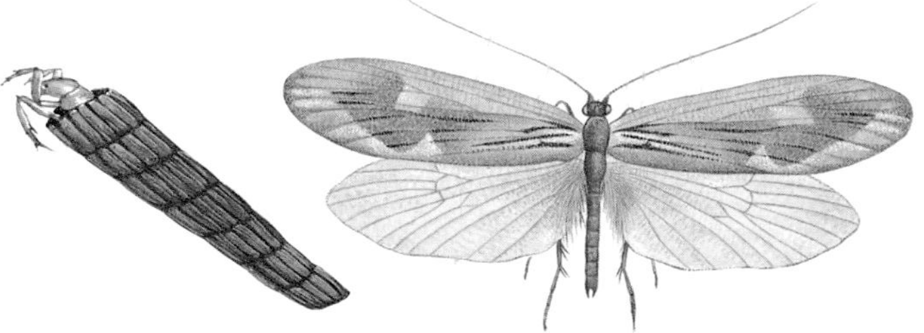

caiman

Caimans are close relatives of ALLIGATORS, and are found in Central and South America. They live in rivers and swamps, and lie in wait for unwary animals, which they drag into the water. The biggest and most dangerous caiman is the black caiman. It can be over 13 feet (4 m) long.

camel

Camels are large desert MAMMALS. They have large feet so they do not sink in sand, and they can go without water for up to five days. A camel's hump stores fat, and the camel uses the fat as an emergency food supply.

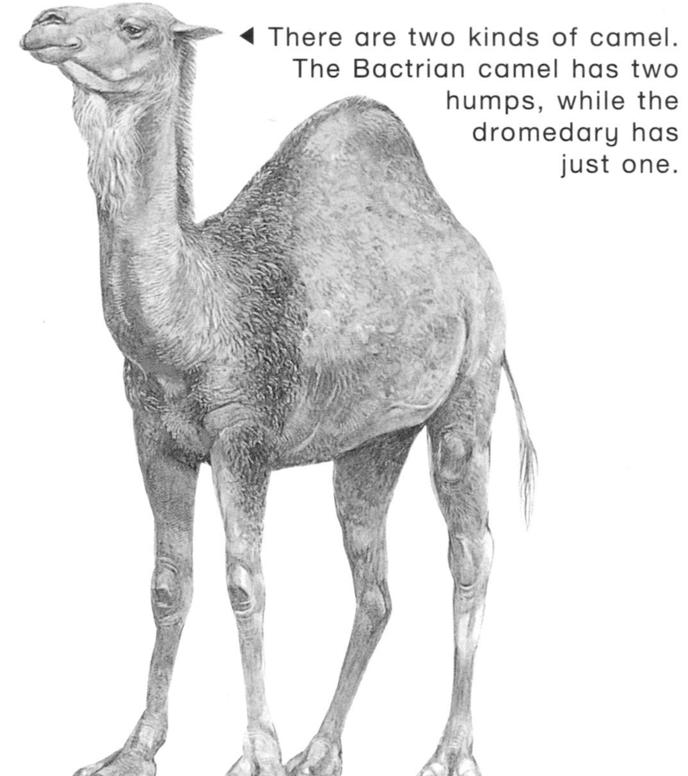

◀ There are two kinds of camel. The Bactrian camel has two humps, while the dromedary has just one.

camouflage see **page 23**

canary

Wild canaries live in the Canary Islands near Africa. These birds are brown or yellow and brown, but pet canaries can be bright yellow. See **domestic animals**.

capybara

The capybara, from South America, is the world's biggest RODENT. A large female can weigh over 110 pounds (50 kg), and can be over a yard (1 m) long. They spend all their time near water, and they feed on grass and water plants, using their sharp teeth. See **coypu**.

CAMOUFLAGE

All animals have to find food, and they also have to avoid being eaten. One of the ways that they do this is by being camouflaged. A camouflaged animal looks just like its background, so that it is very hard to see. Some of the best-camouflaged animals are INSECTS. If you go for a walk in the woods, look very carefully at the tree trunks, and you will probably find camouflaged insects on the bark. Many hunting animals use camouflage to creep up on their prey.

▲ A leaf insect looks almost exactly like a leaf. It even has raised lines that match a leaf's veins.

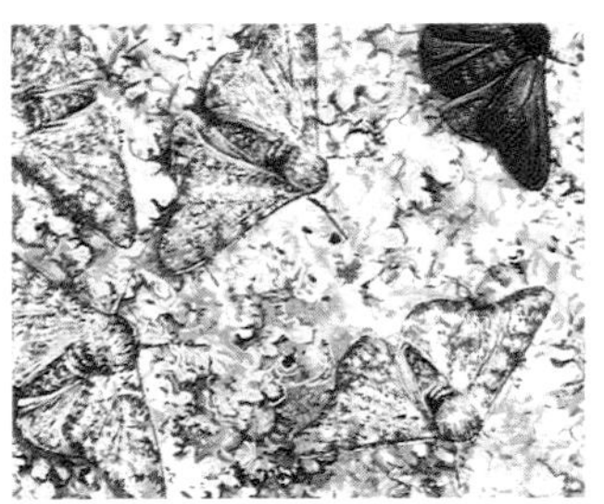

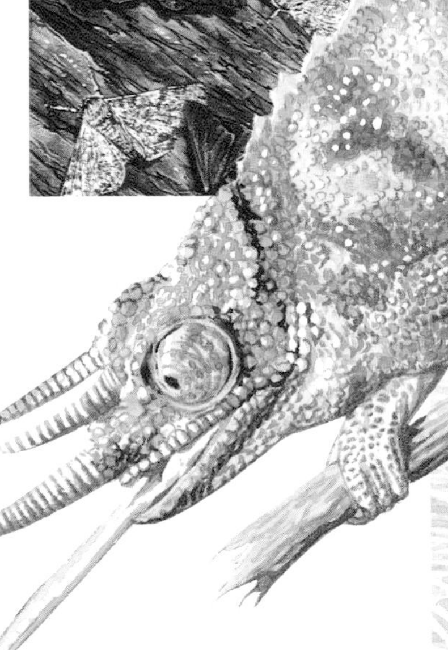

▲ Peppered moths can be light or dark. On a light-colored tree trunk, light moths are camouflaged, but black moths stand out. This means that the black moths are more likely to be spotted and eaten by birds.

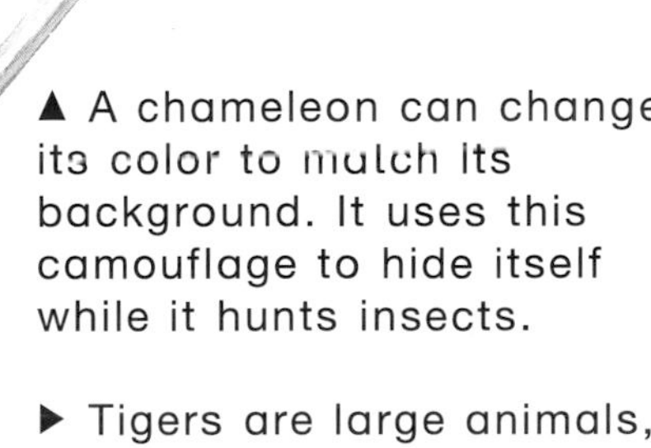

▲ A chameleon can change its color to match its background. It uses this camouflage to hide itself while it hunts insects.

▶ Tigers are large animals, but their stripes help them to hide in the dappled shade of the forest floor. Young deer often have spots which hide them in the same way.

C

caracal

The caracal is a wild relative of the CAT, measuring about 3 feet (1 m). Its ears have furry tufts, and it hunts with its sharp teeth and claws. Caracals live in Africa and Asia, and they feed on small mammals and other animals. See **lynx**.

cardinal

With its bright red body and feathery crest, the male northern cardinal is one of the most beautiful small BIRDS in North America. The female is dull brown, but like the male, she is a good singer.

▲ Cardinals eat insects, seeds, and fruit. They are frequent visitors to bird feeders, particularly in the winter when food is scarce.

carp

The carp is a freshwater FISH that sucks up food from the bottom of rivers and ponds. They have fat bodies and are slow-moving. Carp can live for 40 years.

◀ Carp originally came from Asia, but were introduced into Europe for food long ago. They were kept in ponds and fattened up for eating.

cassowary

Few people have seen a cassowary, because these large flightless BIRDS live deep in the RAIN FOREST of northern Australia and New Guinea. A cassowary is jet black, except for colored skin on its head and neck. Its wings are tiny, and its head has a hard bony crest, which it uses to push through the jungle. An adult cassowary is almost as tall as a person.

cat

Pet cats belong to an animal family that also includes LIONS, TIGERS, and LEOPARDS. All these animals are MAMMALS that live by hunting. They have superb eyesight and hearing, and their front claws can be pulled in when not in use. In places such as Australia, pet cats have caused great damage to local wildlife. The wildcat lives in Europe and Asia. It looks like a pet cat, but it is bigger and has dark rings around its tail. See **bobcat**, **caracal**, **domestic animals**, **lynx**.

▲ Wildcats are never tame. They keep away from people, and hunt birds and other animals.

cavy see **guinea pig**

centipede

Centipedes are fast-moving ARTHROPODS with poisonous claws and up to 300 legs. They are active mainly at night, and they search the ground for insects and other small animals. Most centipedes are harmless to humans, but the giant centipedes of Africa and South America have a dangerous bite. See **millipede**.

chameleon

Chameleons, unlike most LIZARDS, move extremely slowly. They feed on insects, which they catch by shooting out their long sticky tongues. Chameleons can change color to blend into their background, and they can move their eyes in different directions at the same time. Most chameleons live in Africa. See **camouflage**.

chamois

Climbers often wear rubber-soled boots to stop themselves slipping. The nimble chamois lives in the mountains, and its hooves work in just the same way. Chamois are close relatives of GOATS and are about the same size. They live in Europe and Asia, and they feed on mountain plants.

cheetah

The cheetah is the fastest land animal. It can reach a speed of over 60 miles (100 km) per hour. Cheetahs are members of the CAT family, and they live in Africa and Asia. They have light bodies with very long legs, and their backs bend so that they can take huge strides. Unlike LIONS, cheetahs hunt mainly in the open.

chimpanzee

Chimpanzees are our closest relatives in the animal world. Chimps live in forests and open woodlands in Africa. Like most other PRIMATES, they eat many different things, and they even make simple tools to pick insects out of holes and crevices. Chimps are good climbers, but they spend most of their time on the ground.

chinchilla

The chinchilla's fur keeps it warm in the mountains of South America. These RODENTS were once common, but many have been killed, and they are now rare.

▶ Chipmunks carry food back to their burrows in cheek pouches. They are not afraid of people, and often eat leftovers at campsites.

chipmunk

Chipmunks are a type of GROUND SQUIRREL that live in North America and central Asia. They live in burrows under the ground. Chipmunks feed mainly on seeds. In the fall they collect and store lots of food, and use it to survive through the winter, when food is scarce.

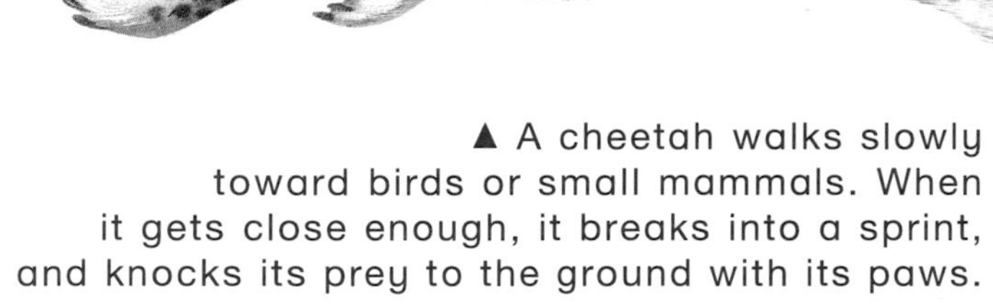

▲ A cheetah walks slowly toward birds or small mammals. When it gets close enough, it breaks into a sprint, and knocks its prey to the ground with its paws.

▶ Male cicadas make a loud clicking sound by squeezing and stretching parts of their bodies.

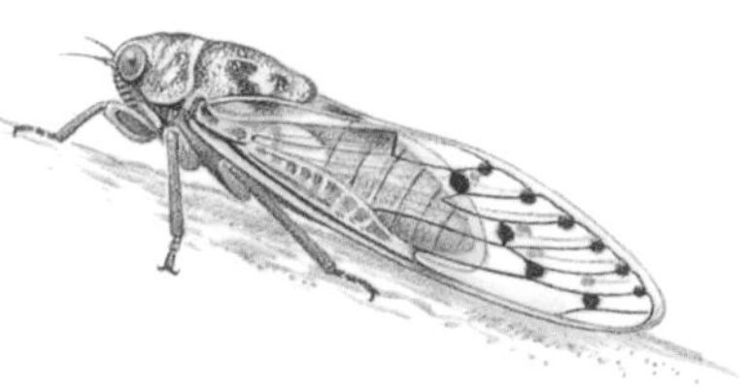

cicada

In many warm parts of the world, the non-stop call of cicadas fills the night with sound. Cicadas are large BUGS that spend most of their lives underground. They dig their way through the soil, and suck sap from plant roots. After several years, the young cicadas make their way to the surface, and change into winged adults.

▼ The giant clam is the largest mollusk that lives inside a shell. It lives in coral reefs in the Indian and Pacific Oceans, and is over a yard across.

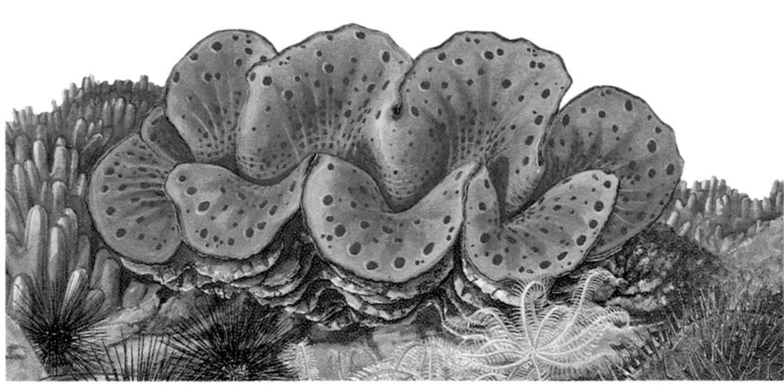

clam

Clams belong to a group of animals called MOLLUSKS. They have soft bodies, but they are protected by a hard shell. Their shells have two halves which can close tightly if danger threatens.

click beetle

If a click beetle is put on its back, it pulls in its legs and keeps still. Then, without warning, it catapults itself into the air emitting a loud click as it does so. Click beetles do this by suddenly bending their bodies. This enables them to escape from predators. See **beetle**.

climbing perch

The climbing perch is a FISH that lives in pools and ditches, where the water often contains very little oxygen. It survives by hauling itself out of the water, and breathing air. Climbing perches can use their strong fins to clamber up branches, or even to move from one pool to another. They live in Asia. See **perch**.

clothes moth

Clothes moths are small golden-brown moths that often live indoors. They are not much bigger than a housefly, and they usually scuttle away from danger, rather than fly off. Clothes moths can be a problem, because their caterpillars feed on natural fibers, such as wool. They can chew holes in woolen clothes and carpets. Humans have accidentally helped clothes moths to spread all over the world. See **butterflies and moths**.

coati

The coati looks like a mixture between a cat and a dog. Coatis are MAMMALS, and are relatives of RACCOONS. They live in the forests of South America, and they use their long, mobile snouts to search out small animals such as insects or lizards.

◀ A coati has a long tail, with dark rings. Coatis live in groups, and they use their tails as a signal.

cobra
Cobras are large and very poisonous SNAKES. Some cobras have long ribs just behind their heads, and they can spread these ribs wide to make a "hood" to scare off enemies. Spitting cobras, which live in Africa, can squirt their poison through the air.

▶ The king cobra is the world's biggest poisonous snake. It eats other snakes, and is a good climber.

cockroach
Cockroaches are fast-moving and unpopular INSECTS. They like warm places, and they often live inside houses. Cockroaches are active at night, and they search for food with their long antennae. They will eat almost anything, from stale bread to soap.

cockatoo
Cockatoos are noisy PARROTS that have long crests on their heads. A cockatoo raises its crest to show its mood. Cockatoos spend much of their time in flocks and all live in Australia or Southeast Asia. The biggest is the black cockatoo, which cracks open hard nuts with its massive curved beak. The sulfur-crested cockatoo is all white, except for its yellow crest.

▲ The galah is a common Australian cockatoo.

cockle
Cockles are MOLLUSKS with furrowed shells made of two parts. They live in muddy sand, and they eat by sieving food from seawater. On many muddy shores, millions of cockles are hidden away just beneath the surface. See **clam**.

cod
The cod is one of the the most important food FISH in the northern hemisphere. It grows to about 3 feet (1 m) long, and lives in shallow water near the coast. A female cod releases millions of eggs into the water, but very few of them survive to become adults.

coelacanth
In 1938, scientists were amazed when a strangely shaped FISH was caught off southern Africa. The fish was a coelacanth. Coelacanths belong to a group of fish that were thought to have died out over 60 million years ago.

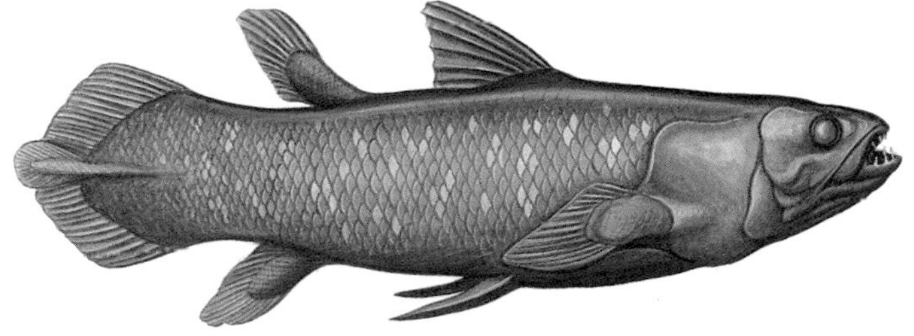
▲ A coelacanth has stubby fins with lobed bases, and a short, blunt tail. It lives in deep and dark water.

C

coelenterates

A coelenterate, or cnidarian, is a simple animal with a hollow body. Its mouth is ringed by tentacles, and it uses the tentacles to catch food. There are over 10,000 kinds of coelenterate, and most of them live in the sea. A coelenterate's tentacles are covered with stinging threads. Some coelenterates, such as the PORTUGUESE MAN-OF-WAR, have such poisonous stinging hairs that they are dangerous to swimmers.

COELENTERATES

Coelenterates all have soft bodies, but some corals protect themselves by making hard cases. These cases sometimes build up to form reefs.

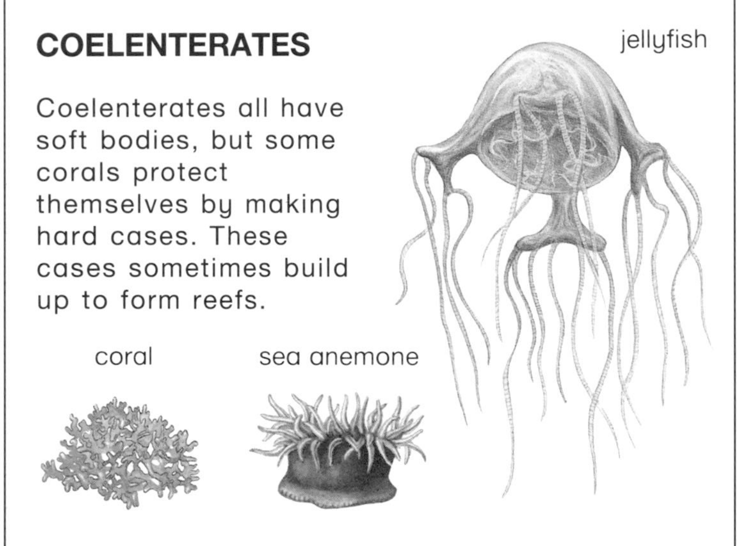

colobus

Colobuses are MONKEYS that live in the dense forests of central Africa. They eat leaves and insects, and are very good climbers, even though they have tiny thumbs, or no thumbs at all. Colobuses live in large groups.

Colorado beetle

The striped black and yellow Colorado beetle is a serious insect pest of potato plants. The beetle and its grubs can ruin a crop. See **beetle**.

communication see **page 29**

▶ The Andean condor from South America is now very rare.

condor

With wingspans of 10 feet (3 m), condors are among the largest flying birds. Condors are VULTURES, and they live in North and South America. They find their food by soaring high over MOUNTAINS, and keeping a watch on the ground far below. The Californian condor, from North America, has become almost extinct. See **birds of prey**.

▶ Colorado beetles are North American, but they have been carried accidentally to other parts of the world. Farmers watch out for these beetles, because they can quickly destroy a whole field of potato plants.

COMMUNICATION

Communication is important to all animals, because it enables one animal to give information to another. We communicate with other people all the time, by talking and making expressions with our faces and bodies. Animals cannot talk to each other, but many use sounds and body movements to get a message across. Many mammals have a good sense of smell, and they communicate by scent. Smell is also important to many insects, such as ants. If an ant has an unfamiliar scent, other ants in a nest will quickly kill it. Some animals also communicate by touch. See **cicada**, **firefly**, **glowworm**, **howler monkey**, **humpback whale**.

▶ Fireflies find a mate by flashing a light on and off.

▼ Song thrushes sing to show that they have claimed a piece of ground.

◀ If it is threatened, a gorilla snarls and shows its teeth. This frightens off most of its enemies.

▶ Lemurs have a good sense of smell. They mark their territories by leaving scent on branches and tree trunks.

▶ Wolves live in groups, and they use facial expressions to communicate with each other. Here, you can see four expressions that carry very different messages.

friendly

playful

ready to defend

ready to attack

conger eel
The conger is one of the world's largest eels, reaching a length of 8 feet (2.5 m). Like other eels it has a snakelike body without a covering of scales. Congers feed on fish and crabs, crushing them with their powerful jaws. They live throughout the North Atlantic. See **eel**, **fish**.

▼ The conger feeds at night. During the day, it hides away in crevices.

coniferous forests see **pages 32 and 33**

conservation see **pages 34 and 35**

coot
The coot is a small black BIRD that lives on ponds and lakes in many different parts of the world. Coots feed mainly on plants and insects, although they sometimes eat eggs and even young birds.

coral
Corals are COELENTERATES. A coral has a short stumpy body and its mouth is surrounded by a ring of stinging tentacles. Corals live in the sea, and they catch tiny animals to eat by trailing their tentacles in the water. Some corals build hard cases for protection. Over many years, these cases can build up into underwater walls called coral reefs. The world's biggest reef is the Great Barrier Reef, off northeast Australia. It is over 1,200 miles (2,000 km) long.

cormorant
Cormorants are black or black-and-white seabirds that feed on fish. They catch their food by paddling underwater and can dive to 100 feet (30 m) or more.

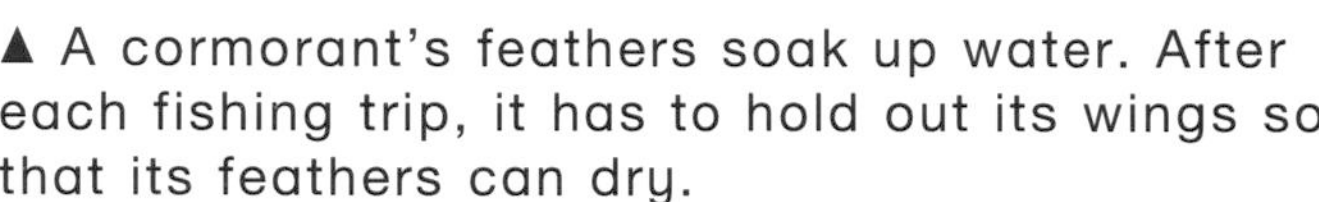

▲ A cormorant's feathers soak up water. After each fishing trip, it has to hold out its wings so that its feathers can dry.

courtship see **behavior**

coyote
Coyotes are members of the DOG family that live all across North America, from the Alaskan tundra to the deserts of Mexico. Like foxes, they eat a wide range of food, including fruit, insects, small mammals, and even snakes.

▶ Coyotes hunt mainly at night, and their loud calls can be heard a long way off. They bring up their young in burrows, and can have as many as 12 pups at one time.

coypu
The coypu is a large RODENT from South America. It feeds on plants, and it rarely strays far from water. Coypus are sometimes bred for their soft fur.

crab

Crabs are CRUSTACEANS, and their bodies are covered by hard plates. A crab has 10 legs, and it normally moves sideways. Two of the legs end in pincers, and the crab uses these for feeding or for fending off attackers. Crabs feed on small plants and the remains of dead animals. Some spend their whole lives in water, but others come out of the water to feed.

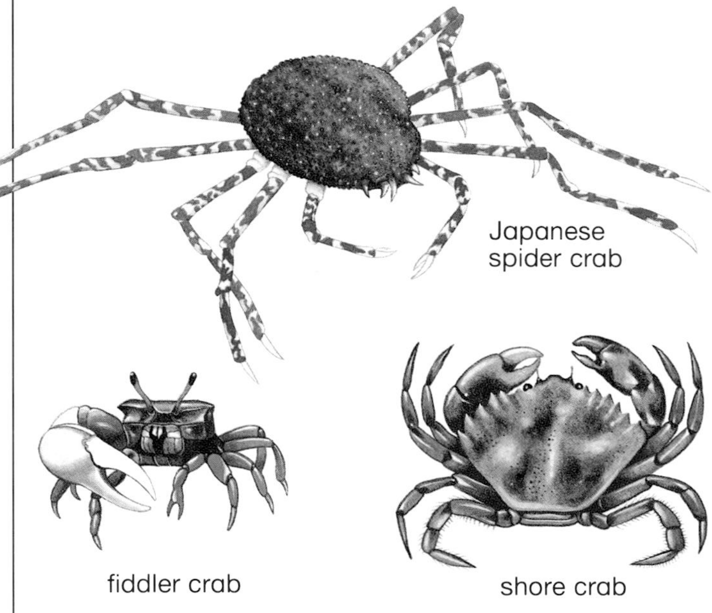

▲ The Japanese spider crab measures over 10 feet (3 m) when stretched out. Crabs that live near the shore are much smaller.

crab spider

Crab spiders do not make webs to catch food. Instead, they lurk on or underneath flowers, and wait for visiting insects. When an insect lands on the flower, a crab spider rushes out and injects it with a deadly poison. Most crab spiders are brightly colored. See **spider**.

crane

Cranes are tall birds with long legs and necks. They usually live in wet places or on open grassland. Cranes feed on seeds, fruit, and small animals. During the breeding season, they dance by leaping high into the air and flapping their wings. Cranes can live to be over 50, which is very old for a bird.

cricket

Crickets are heavy-bodied jumping INSECTS that live all over the world, except in very cold places. They have long antennae, or feelers, and they spend most of their time slowly clambering over the ground, or up plants. Crickets eat plants or insects. The males can make loud sounds by scraping their forewings together. Some crickets can fly. See **grasshopper**.

crocodile

Crocodiles are large and dangerous REPTILES that spend their lives in or near water. Like their close relatives, the ALLIGATORS, crocodiles have armored skin and large teeth, and they hunt by pulling their prey underwater. A female crocodile lays eggs in a hole in sandy ground, and when the young crocodiles hatch she carefully carries them to water in her huge jaws. See **caimans**.

▼ There are 13 different kinds of crocodile, and the biggest can grow up to 20 feet (6 m) long. Crocodiles spend much of their time lazing on muddy banks close to the water.

CONIFEROUS FORESTS

Conifers are trees that grow their seeds in cones. They are good at coping with cold weather, and in the far north they form a huge forest that stretches almost all the way around the world. Most conifers have narrow leaves called needles, and they usually keep them in winter. Their branches slope downward so that snow can slide off. The inside of a coniferous forest is often dark. ANTS roam the forest floor, and in some places BEARS wander among the trees, looking for all kinds of food, from birds to honey. Many more animals live high up in the trees. They include SAWFLIES, whose caterpillars feed on pine needles, and ICHNEUMONS. The treetops make a home for many birds. CROSSBILLS pick seeds out of cones, and WOODPECKERS probe the tree trunks for insects.

NORTHERN FORESTS IN DANGER

Coniferous forests make up the biggest forests in the world. Although they grow more slowly than tropical forests, they are still packed with wildlife. Unfortunately for forest animals, coniferous trees are a valuable source of timber. In some parts of the northern hemisphere, entire forests are cut down so that their timber can be used to make things. When this happens, young trees are often planted.

▼ This forest is typical of the forests found in North America. European coniferous forests have different animals.

MINIBEASTS OF CONIFEROUS FORESTS

Insects are very important in coniferous forests. They feed on wood and leaves, or on each other. Some beetles chew their way through dead wood, and ants collect dead leaves and use them for their nests. The caterpillars of moths and butterflies often feed on living leaves, and the larvae of wood wasps feed on living wood. Ichneumons lay their eggs in or on the grubs of other insects.

FOREST LIFE

1 Marten
2 Blackburnian warbler
3 Ruby-crowned kinglet
4 Crossbill
5 Brown bear
6 Wolverine
7 Moose
8 Long-eared owl
9 Gray squirrel
10 Pileated woodpecker
11 Lynx
12 Chipmunk
13 Osprey
14 Porcupine

▼ Northern coniferous forests have cold winters. Some of the animals spend the coldest months in hibernation. Small insect-eating birds like the blackburnian warbler fly away to warmer places.

CONSERVATION

There are over 5 billion people on Earth, and the human population is still growing fast. Humans need space to live and to grow food, and the more space that we take up, the less there is for wild animals. Conservation means helping wildlife to survive in our changing world. Sometimes, particular animals can be helped by protecting them from hunting, or moving them from places where they are threatened. But the most effective kind of conservation involves protecting entire habitats, so that all the animals that live there can survive.

▶Tropical rain forests are the richest wildlife habitats on land. But every year, huge areas of them are cut down to make way for farming. Half of the world's tropical rain forests have already been destroyed, and if they continue to be cleared at this rate, there will soon be none left. For animals like the golden lion tamarin and morpho butterfly, this means disaster. Once the forests have gone, they cannot survive.

◀ The grasslands of North America were once the home of over 50 million bison. When Europeans began to settle in the Midwest, hunters killed bison in great numbers. In less than 50 years, hardly any bison were left. The North American passenger pigeon was once the world's most numerous bird, and lived in flocks over a billion strong. Hunters wiped them out, and the last passenger pigeon died in a zoo in 1914.

▶ Humans have taken cats, rats, and goats all over the world. These animals often make life hard for the wildlife around them. Flightless birds, such as the kakapo from New Zealand, are endangered by rats that eat their eggs and young. The giant weta is also under threat in New Zealand. Plant-eaters, like the giant tortoises from the Galapagos Islands, risk starvation if goats eat all their food.

◀ The Mediterranean monk seal was once common in the Mediterranean, but it is now very rare. Like many sea animals, it cannot cope with polluted water, motorboats, and busy beaches. Turtles also struggle to survive in vacation areas. They lay their eggs at night on sandy beaches, but they are easily put off by the noise and the bright lights of seaside hotels.

CAN YOU HELP?

The world's wildlife faces great problems, and it is easy to think that there is nothing you can do about it. But if everybody helps in a small way, things can get better. You can help animals by persuading people not to wear fur coats. You can help to reduce waste by not buying things that are over-packaged.

C

crossbill

The crossbill is a small BIRD with a very unusual beak. Instead of meeting at a point, the beak's upper and lower tips cross over. The crossbill eats the seeds of coniferous trees such as pines, and it uses its beak to lever the seeds out of cones growing on the trees.

▶ Crows often live on farmland, and they sometimes come into gardens. Many people do not like crows because they often eat the nestlings of other birds.

crow

Crows are large black BIRDS with strong beaks. Compared to most birds they are quite intelligent, and they are quick to spot the chance of a meal. Crows feed on small animals, crops, and our leftovers. They live in many parts of the world.

crustaceans

Crustaceans are ARTHROPODS that have a hard body case, or crust. They include CRABS, LOBSTERS and SHRIMPS, and also animals called water fleas. Crustaceans have many pairs of legs, and they often have pincers. Most crustaceans live in the sea, and many spend the early part of their lives floating in the top layers of the water. As a crustacean grows up, it changes shape, and it often settles on the shore, or on the seabed. The WOOD LOUSE is one of the few crustaceans that live on land. See **barnacle**.

cuckoo

The cuckoo is a remarkable European BIRD that tricks other birds into raising its young. A female cuckoo searches out the nests of WARBLERS and other small birds. When she finds a nest, she lays a single egg and then quickly flies off. The egg soon hatches, and the young cuckoo pushes the other nestlings out of the nest. The foster parents spend all their time collecting enough food for the cuckoo to eat.

curlew

Curlews are brown BIRDS that live in damp places throughout Asia and Africa. They have long legs and extremely long curved beaks. The curlew's beak is a perfect tool for finding small animals that are buried in soft mud.

cuttlefish

Cuttlefish are MOLLUSKS that live on the sea floor in shallow water. Like the OCTOPUS and SQUID, they catch animals using their sucker-bearing tentacles. A cuttlefish can change its color within seconds to match its background. See **camouflage**.

CRUSTACEANS

A crustacean's hard body protects it from its enemies. Crabs and lobsters are the largest crustaceans, and they live in the sea.

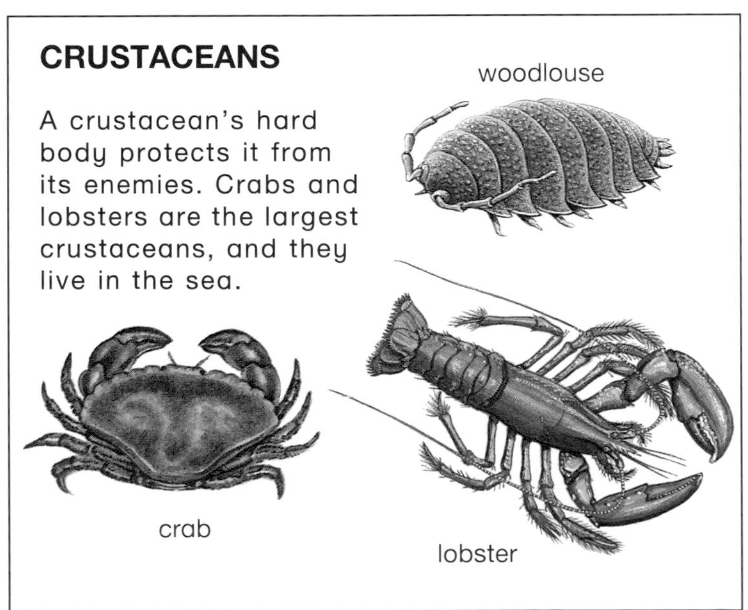

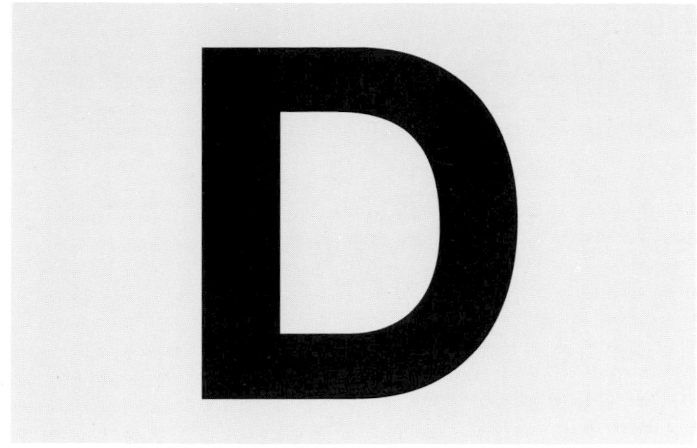

deathwatch beetle
Deathwatch beetles feed on wood. Normally they live inside trees, but sometimes they feed inside the timbers of very old houses. Deathwatch beetles slowly chew through house timbers, and they can make them so weak that they collapse. See **beetle**.

◀ Deathwatch beetles signal to each other by tapping their heads against the wood. This sound is easiest to hear at night, when the rest of a house is quiet.

deciduous forests see **pages 38 and 39**

deer
Deer are hoofed MAMMALS or UNGULATES that have long necks and slender legs. They feed on grass, leaves, and bark. Most male deer have antlers. Antlers look like horns, but they are made of bone. See **moose**, **reindeer**.

defense see **page 40**

deserts see **pages 42 and 43**

dingo
The dingo is a sandy-colored DOG that lives in the deserts and bush of Australia. Dingos are hunters. They feed on many kinds of animals, from rabbits to large marsupials. They also attack sheep. See **domestic animals**.

dipper
The dipper is a small, plump BIRD with a very unusual way of feeding. It jumps into streams, and walks or swims underwater, looking for insects and other water animals. Dippers live by clean, fast-flowing streams in North America, Europe, and Asia, and they often have nests behind waterfalls.

dog
The dogs that people keep as pets belong to a family of MAMMALS that includes COYOTES, WOLVES, and FOXES. In the wild, all these animals live by hunting. They have long jaws with big teeth, and they find their prey mainly by using their sense of smell, which is far better than ours. The first pet dogs probably looked quite like wolves. After thousands of years of breeding, there are now many different kinds of pet dog. See **domestic animals**.

▼ Dogs vary enormously in appearance. Some dogs are tiny, like the chihuahua, which is smaller than a rabbit, and others are very tall.

D

DECIDUOUS FORESTS

Many parts of the world have warm summers but quite cold winters. These are the places where deciduous forests grow. In a deciduous forest, the trees drop their leaves before the cold weather begins. If you visit a deciduous forest in winter, it may seem empty and lifeless, with only a few birds and mammals on the lookout for food. But as spring approaches, the forest suddenly begins to change. Plants burst into life on the forest floor, and leaves start to appear on the trees. Now there is lots of food for plant-eating animals, and the forest comes alive.

WOODLANDS IN DANGER?

Deciduous woodlands once covered almost the whole of western Europe. Much of this woodland has been cut down, but there are still some places left where woodlands have stood for thousands of years. These ancient woodlands contain large, old trees and rare insects. As towns and cities grow, these remaining woods are threatened.

WOODLAND LIFE

1 Green woodpecker
2 Red fox
3 Jay
4 Sparrowhawk
5 Wild boar
6 Nuthatch
7 Wood pigeon
8 Red squirrel
9 Brown creeper
10 Hedgehog
11 Polecat
12 Fallow deer
13 Wood mouse
14 Badger
15 Purple emperor butterfly
16 Lesser spotted woodpecker

NORTH AMERICAN WOODLANDS

Deciduous woodland covers a large part of eastern North America, and is famous for its beautiful fall colors. These forests are the home of raccoons and skunks, and also of white-tailed deer. In summer, huge numbers of warblers arrive from the south to raise their families. The blue jay eats insects and nuts. In winter it often visits yards to feed at bird tables.

▼ Deciduous trees provide food for many kinds of animal. Insects and deer feed on their leaves, while jays, woodpeckers, and squirrels eat their seeds. Badgers and wild boars find plenty of food on the woodland floor.

DEFENSE

For most animals, every day brings the risk of being attacked and eaten. To survive, an animal has to be able to defend itself. Defense often means being alert and being ready to make a quick getaway. For example, small birds always watch out for trouble, and so too do most plant-eating animals, such as RABBITS and ANTELOPES. But some animals do not run away from danger. Instead, they hold their ground and try to frighten their enemies away. Other animals defend themselves by attacking back. Some animals taste unpleasant, so that if an enemy does eat one of them, it is unlikely to try another. See **behavior**, **camouflage**.

▶ A skunk defends itself by squirting a horrible-smelling liquid at its attacker. The skunk's stripes warn that it has this special weapon.

▲ A frilled lizard bluffs its way out of trouble by raising special folds of skin.

▼ A hedgehog reacts to danger by rolling into a ball. The soft parts of its body are tucked away, and its sharp spines make it difficult to attack.

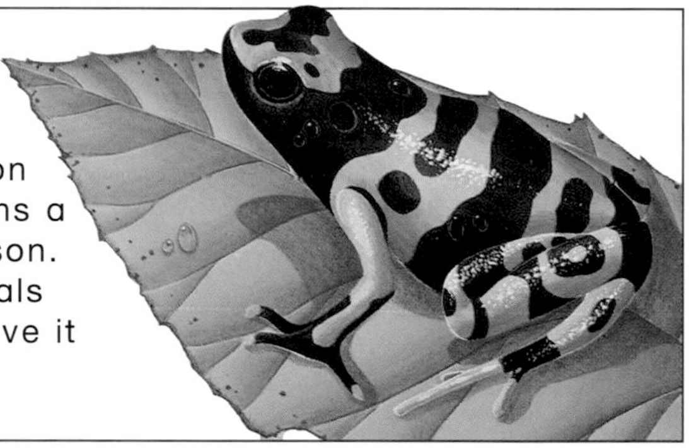

▶ The tiny arrow poison frog contains a deadly poison. Other animals learn to leave it alone.

▼ If wolves attack, musk oxen defend their calves by standing in a circle, with their horns facing outward.

D

dolphin
A dolphin is a small WHALE with a domed head and a narrow jaw, like a beak. Dolphins feed on fish, and they find their prey in the same way as BATS, by sending out bursts of high-pitched sound, and then listening for the echoes that bounce back. Dolphins are extremely intelligent. Scientists have found that they "talk" to each other by making clicking and whistling noises, and they often hunt together in well-organized groups. Dolphins live in oceans all over the world, and they can often be seen breaking through the surface or riding the waves in front of moving boats.

▲ Like whales, dolphins breathe air. When a baby dolphin is born, it is helped to the surface by its mother so that it can take its first breath.

domestic animals see **page 44**

dormouse
The dormouse is a small, bushy-tailed RODENT that spends up to half the year in a deep winter sleep. Dormice live in woods in Europe and Asia. During the summer and fall they eat lots of seeds and fruit, and they store extra food in a special nest made of moss and leaves. When winter begins, a dormouse curls up inside its nest, and begins to HIBERNATE.

dragonfly
Dragonflies are fast-flying INSECTS that swoop on other insects in midair. An adult dragonfly has a long body and two pairs of transparent wings. Its large eyes can quickly spot any food.

◀ Dragonflies live all over the world near damp places. Young dragonflies grow up in ponds. They catch small animals in their special pincers that shoot forward.

duck
Ducks are BIRDS that are specially shaped for life on water. They have webbed feet and broad, flat beaks, and they keep their feathers waterproof with a special oil. Ducks feed in several different ways. Some of them scoop small plants and animals from the water's surface, while others dive down into the water and collect food from the bottom.

dugong see **sea cow**

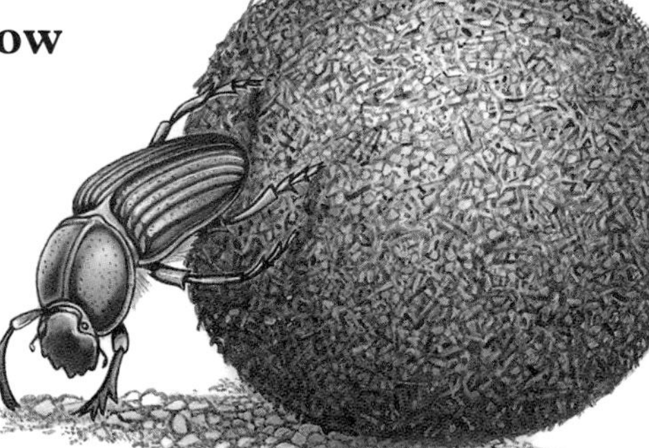

▶ This dung beetle is about to bury a ball of dung. By doing this, dung beetles help to break down animal droppings, and fertilize the soil.

dung beetle
When a dung beetle finds some droppings, it pats them into a ball, and then rolls the ball away by pushing with its back legs. It buries the ball in a small burrow, and lays some eggs on it. When the beetle's grubs hatch, they have a ready-made supply of food. See **beetle**.

EXPANDING DESERTS

Today, the Sahara is dry and barren. Hundreds of years ago, the same area was covered with wooded grassland where people lived and hunted wild animals. The climate then changed, and the plants slowly died out in a battle against drought. Deserts are still growing in many parts of the world, from India to Australia.

DESERT LIFE

1 Bobcat
2 Jackrabbit
3 Kangaroo rat
4 Rattlesnake
5 Kit fox
6 Pack rat
7 Collared lizard
8 Scorpion
9 Gila monster
10 Peccary
11 Spotted skunk
12 Elf owl

DESERTS

Deserts are difficult places for animals to live in. They are very dry, so few plants manage to grow. The days can be very hot, but at night the temperature can plunge below freezing. Sometimes the wind blows fiercely for days on end, and there are few places to shelter from it. Despite this, some animals thrive in deserts. Many of them spend the day underground, and come to the surface at night. Although most small desert mammals are active at night, desert reptiles often hunt by day.

◀ A cactus makes an ideal shelter for the elf owl. It nests in saguaro cacti, using holes pecked out by woodpeckers. The saguaro's flowers provide sugary nectar that is eaten by bats and insects.

LIVING WITHOUT WATER

In most deserts the rain usually comes in sudden downpours that can be many months apart. This means that desert animals have to cope with very little water. Some insects drink the dew that forms during cool desert nights. Jerboas and gerbils get water from their food, and the oryx does the same. A camel has to drink, but it loses body water very slowly. It can drink enough water to last up to 5 days.

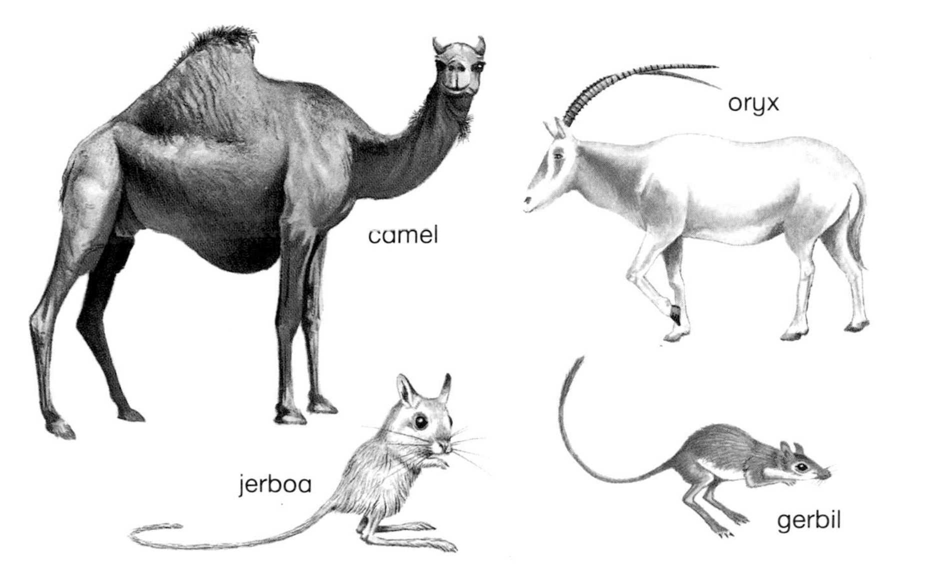

DOMESTIC ANIMALS

DOGS, CATS, and cattle are all examples of domestic animals. Instead of living in the wild, they live either in our houses, or on farms. We keep some domestic animals as pets, and others provide us with food or wool. Before cars and trucks were invented, domestic animals such as HORSES, CAMELS, and LLAMAS were also used to carry loads from place to place. Animals become domesticated by growing up close to humans, so that they become tame. Dogs were probably the first animals to be domesticated, at least 12,000 years ago. Cats have been domesticated for about 6,000 years.

▼ There are many different breeds of dog. The labrador is very placid, and makes a good guide dog. There are different cat breeds, but most are similar in size.

◀ At one time, domestic animals were the only way of carrying heavy loads. These load carriers include horses, mules, and llamas, and also camels and Asiatic elephants.

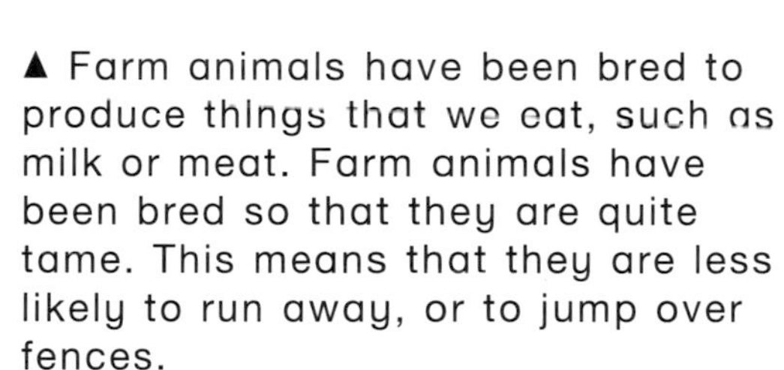

▲ Farm animals have been bred to produce things that we eat, such as milk or meat. Farm animals have been bred so that they are quite tame. This means that they are less likely to run away, or to jump over fences.

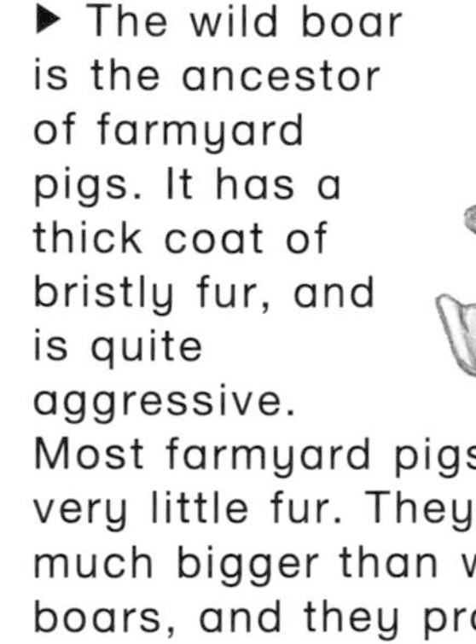

▶ The wild boar is the ancestor of farmyard pigs. It has a thick coat of bristly fur, and is quite aggressive. Most farmyard pigs have very little fur. They are much bigger than wild boars, and they produce more piglets every year.

eagle

Eagles are strong, heavily built BIRDS OF PREY that have powerful talons and hooked beaks. Most eagles, such as the GOLDEN EAGLE and the South American harpy eagle, feed on mammals and other birds. Somc eagles feed on fish.

earthworm

Earthworms play an important role in the living world by eating their way through the soil. As they burrow underground, they digest the tiny particles of food that the soil contains.

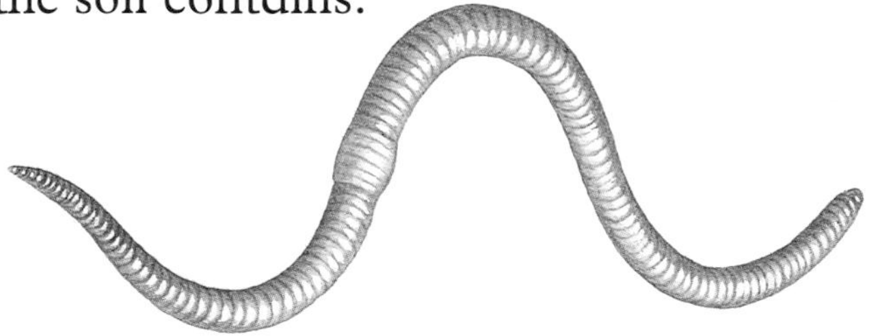

▲ An earthworm has a tubelike body, made of many similar pieces. It spends nearly all its life underground in the dark, but comes to the surface to find a mate.

earwig

Earwigs are INSECTS that have small pincers at the end of their bodies. During the daytime they hide in dark crevices, and they probably got their name because it was thought they could crawl into the ears of sleeping people.

echidna

Also known as spiny ANTEATERS, echidnas are egg-laying MAMMALS. They live in New Guinea and Australia, and they feed on ants and termites, which they suck up through a long tubular snout. Their bodies are covered in spines for protection. See **platypus**.

ECHINODERMS

The echinoderms are a group of animals that includes the sea urchins, sand dollars, and starfish. They creep about using hundreds of small feet.

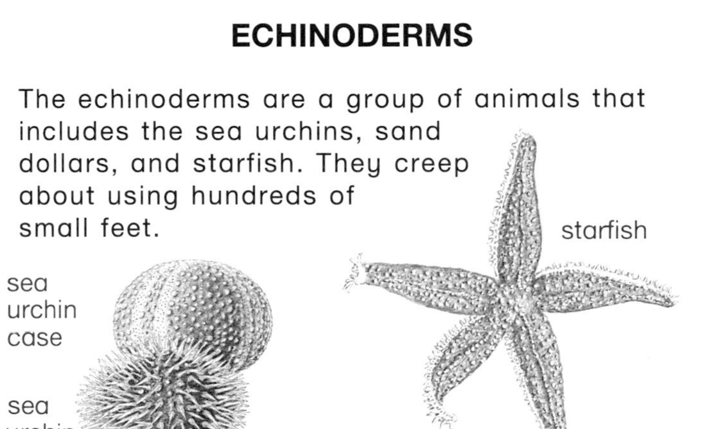

echinoderms

Echinoderms all live in the sea. They have a thin outer body case made of small hard plates. Hundreds of tiny "tube feet" stick through holes in the case, and an echinoderm uses these like suction pads to cling to surfaces or to move around. Echinoderms eat many different kinds of food, from small particles that drift in the water to MOLLUSKS.

▶ Earwigs hunt tiny animals after dark. They use their pincers to catch their prey.

E

eel

There are over 600 different kinds of eel around the world. These long-bodied FISH look quite like snakes, and unlike other fish, they do not have scales. Some eels spend their entire lives in the sea. Others live in rivers but return to the sea to lay their eggs. See **fresh water, migration**.

eider

This large DUCK has given its name to eiderdowns, which were once stuffed with its feathers. The eider lives in the cold waters of the far north, and its feathers are exceptionally dense and warm. Eiders feed on crabs and other small animals.

◀ Eider ducks breed on the coast. The female plucks feathers from her breast and uses them to line her nest.

eland

The eland is the largest of the ANTELOPES. A mature male eland is as large as a farmyard bull, and it has impressive horns twisted into a spiral. Eland live in eastern and southern Africa.

electric eel

Several fish can generate electricity to stun their prey, but the electric eel produces powerful shocks of up to 500 volts. It grows up to 6 feet (2 m) long and is found in South America. See **eel**.

elephant

There are two kinds of elephant, and they live in different parts of the world. The African elephant is the largest land MAMMAL. The Asian elephant, which is found in India, Sri Lanka, and parts of Southeast Asia, is smaller, and has much smaller ears. Both kinds of elephant live in GRASSY PLAINS or forests. They feed on plants which they gather with their trunks.

▲ A male African elephant can be 13 feet (4 m) tall at the shoulder, and can weigh nearly 13,000 pounds (6,000 kg). These huge animals are often hunted for their valuable tusks.

elephant seal

Elephant seals live mainly off the coasts of North and South America. Their young are born on special breeding beaches. Males fight for territories on these beaches. See **seal**.

emu

Emus are long-legged Australian BIRDS that are related to the OSTRICHES of Africa. Like ostriches they are flightless, but they can run very quickly, sometimes reaching nearly 30 miles (50 km) an hour. Emus raid crops and waterholes, and farmers consider them to be a pest. Berries and insects make up most of their diet.

E

EVOLUTION

Evolution is a very gradual change in a living thing's characteristics as onc generation follows another. The main force driving evolution is thought to be natural selection. This occurs because all living things have different characteristics, and some are better suited to the world around them than others. The successful animals leave more descendants, and so their particular characteristics gradually become more common. The first living things on Earth were simple microbes, similar to living bacteria. From these first cells, all forms of life—including plants and animals—have appeared through evolution.

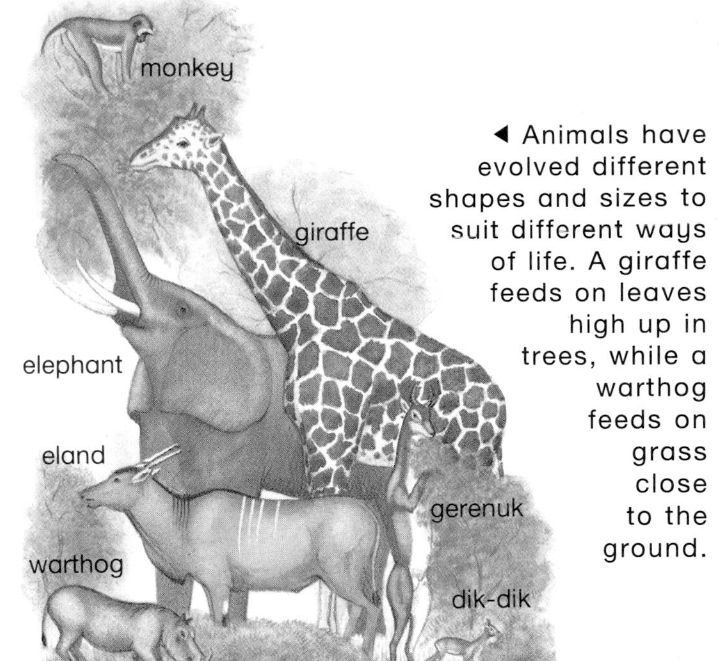

◀ Animals have evolved different shapes and sizes to suit different ways of life. A giraffe feeds on leaves high up in trees, while a warthog feeds on grass close to the ground.

◀ The tuatara is an evolutionary "leftover"—the last surviving member of a group of reptiles that has almost died out.

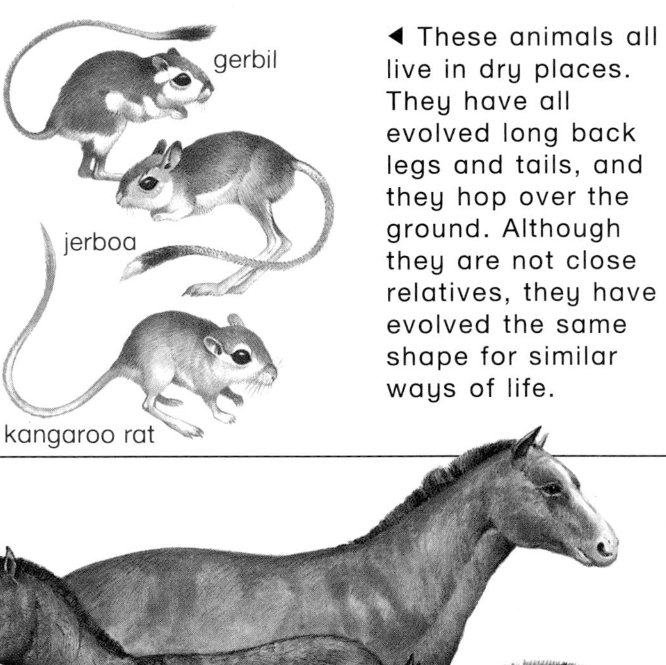

◀ These animals all live in dry places. They have all evolved long back legs and tails, and they hop over the ground. Although they are not close relatives, they have evolved the same shape for similar ways of life.

▶ Evolution does not always run in the same direction. The first reptiles to evolve were land animals. Many of their descendants adapted to life in water. This is *Elasmosaurus*, an extinct swimming reptile.

▲ Horses were not always as big and strong as they are today. The first horses were no bigger than dogs. The horse has slowly become larger during the course of evolution.

falcon
Falcons are small or medium-sized BIRDS OF PREY. Unlike most EAGLES and HAWKS, their wings are sharply pointed, and they often catch their prey in a high-speed chase. The largest falcons hunt mammals and birds, while the smallest live on insects. See **kestrel**, **peregrine**.

feeding see **page 49**

fennec fox
Fennec foxes are not much bigger than a cat. They live in the DESERTS of North Africa and the Middle East, and hunt for mice, lizards, birds, and insects after dark. During the heat of the day they rest in burrows in the sand. Their huge ears help them to hunt. See **fox**.

▼ The fennec fox's big ears help it to hear small animals when it hunts after dark.

fer-de-lance
The fer-de-lance belongs to a family of SNAKES called vipers. It is found in Central and South America, and grows to over 6 feet (2 m). The fer-de-lance has a highly poisonous bite.

ferret
Ferrets are domesticated MAMMALS that have long supple bodies, short legs, long necks, and bright alert eyes. They are probably descended from the European POLECAT, and they are kept to hunt rats and rabbits. They are only partially tame, and they often escape into the wild.

◀ A male fighting fish drives an intruder out of his territory.

fighting fish
Often known as Siamese fighting fish, these small freshwater fish have very large and beautiful fins. During the breeding season, males claim territories and mates, and are always on the alert to drive away intruders. See **behavior**.

finch
Finches are a large group of BIRDS found in most parts of the world. They are generally small and feed on seeds, and they often fly in flocks. Finches that eat small seeds have slender pointed beaks. Those that eat large seeds or nuts have stronger beaks, which work like pliers.

FEEDING

All animals need to take in food, and they get their food in a variety of ways. Many animals feed entirely on plants. They are called herbivores. Although plants are easy to find, they can be difficult to digest. Some plant-eaters, such as RUMINANTS and RABBITS, have special microbes in their stomachs, which do the digesting for them. Meat is much easier to digest, but meat-eaters, or carnivores, often spend much more energy catching their food. Meat-eaters have very sharp senses to detect prey.

◄ A giraffe reaches for leaves high above the ground. Its mouth and tongue are very tough, and are not harmed by the trees' sharp thorns.

▼ Hummingbirds live on nectar—a sugary fluid that is produced by flowers.

◄ An anaconda needs only a few meals a year. It takes many days to digest its food.

◄ As soon as an insect flies into the web, the spider rushes out to eat it.

◄ Many animals that live in the sea filter food from the water. A mussel pumps water over its gills, and these work like a sieve.

▼ Hyenas, jackals, and vultures live on food left behind by other hunters. A hyena can digest all the leftovers, including bones.

firefly

Fireflies are not true flies but small BEETLES that are related to the GLOWWORM. Fireflies produce a chemical reaction in their bodies to make light, which they use to attract a mate. The males flash their lights on and off, and the wingless females flash back so that the males can find them in the dark.

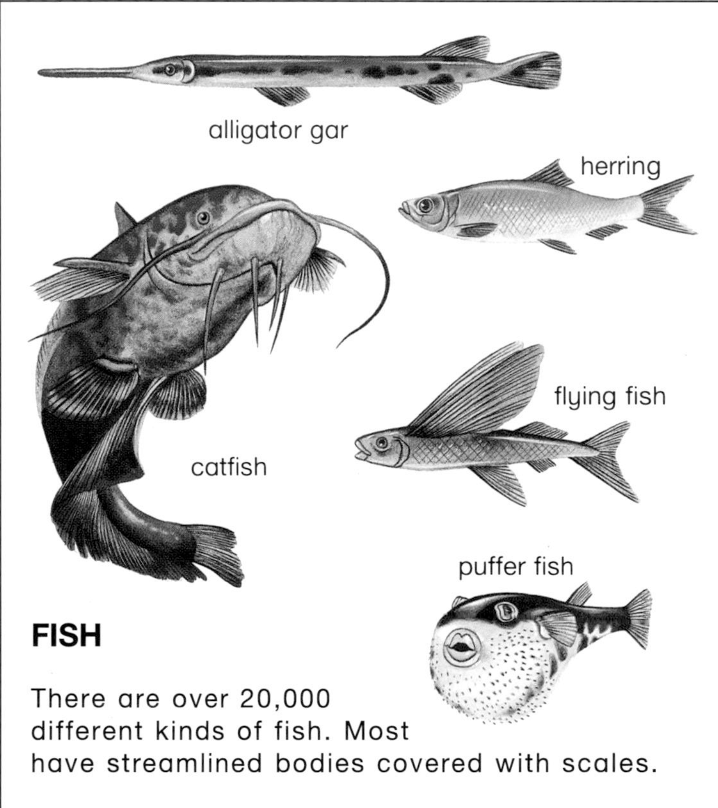

FISH

There are over 20,000 different kinds of fish. Most have streamlined bodies covered with scales.

fish

Fish live in oceans, lakes, and rivers all over the world. There are two major groups of fish, the cartilaginous fish and the bony fish. Cartilaginous fish include the SHARKS and RAYS. Their skeletons are not made of bone, but of a strong, rubbery material called cartilage. Bony fish do have bones, and they include most of the fish alive today. Most fish reproduce by laying eggs, but some of them give birth to live young.

▼ Flamingoes often rest on one leg. When they fly, their legs trail behind their tails.

flamingo

These BIRDS are found in Africa, some southern areas of Europe, western Asia, South America, and the Caribbean. They feed on tiny water plants and animals, and they get their pink color from some of the animals that they eat. Flamingoes feed by dipping their beaks into the water, and waving them from side to side. As they move along, they scoop up water, and then filter it through a sievelike structure in their beaks.

flatfish

When just hatched, a flatfish swims in open water. But as it grows up, it begins to change shape. Its body becomes very flattened, and it spends all its time lying on one side on the seabed. For its own safety, the side facing upward becomes dark and camouflaged, while the underside turns pale. The eye that is underneath slowly moves across its head, so that both eyes eventually point upward. See **halibut**, **plaice**.

flea

Fleas are tiny, blood-sucking PARASITES that live on mammals and birds. They do not have wings, but they can jump a long way using their powerful back legs. Fleas lay their eggs in an animal's nest or lair, and the eggs hatch into tiny thread-like grubs. After a while the grubs turn into adults and jump onto their hosts.

fly

Most flying INSECTS have four wings, but flies have only two. The other pair have evolved to become like tiny knobs, and the fly uses them to keep its balance in the air. Flies are found all over the world, and they live on many different things. Some eat pollen or nectar from flowers, while many are troublesome pests that suck blood from other animals. Flies start life as small grubs that are often called maggots. See **hover fly**, **mosquito**.

▶ Many flies feed by dissolving their food with saliva. They then suck up the liquid that is produced.

flying fish

These small FISH are found in the surface waters of warm oceans. A flying fish can launch itself from the water at high speed, using powerful muscles, and it then opens out its front fins. Using these as wings, it can glide along through the air for up to 300 feet (90 m), before plunging into the waves again. Flying fish glide to escape from predators. They can stay out of the water for only about 10 seconds.

▼ A flying fox's wingspan can reach 6 feet (2 m). It has a long tongue and sharp teeth.

flying fox

Although they look like foxes with wings, flying foxes are actually BATS that live in the tropics and feed on fruit. Flying foxes set off for the fruiting trees at dusk and have very large eyes so that they can see in the dim light. Unlike insect-eating bats, they do not use sound to find their food.

fox

Foxes are carnivorous MAMMALS that eat a wide variety of food, including small rodents, rabbits, birds, insects, and earthworms. Red foxes will also rummage for food in garbage cans. Foxes have a reputation for great intelligence and cunning, and they survive in a very wide range of climates. The small-eared, white-coated Arctic fox lives in icy TUNDRA, while the FENNEC FOX is found in the Sahara.

fresh water see **pages 52 and 53**

frigate bird

These beautiful, slender-winged BIRDS inhabit tropical and subtropical oceans, where they soar high over the water, looking for squid, fish, shrimps, and jellyfish. See **open seas**.

FRESH WATER

Rivers, streams, ponds, and lakes all contain fresh water, rather than the salty water that is found in seas and estuaries. The smallest freshwater animals live on tiny floating plants. They include CRUSTACEANS, such as tiny water fleas, and also the AMOEBAS. Fresh water is also the home of the young, or larvae, of many INSECTS. Freshwater FISH feed on these small animals, and they in turn are the food of larger animals. HERONS patiently stalk fish at the water's edge, and KINGFISHERS dive for fish near the surface. Some freshwater animals use the water only at certain times of the year. FROGS and TOADS return to fresh water in spring to lay their eggs, and their tadpoles grow up there, leaving in the late summer.

THREATENED WETLANDS

Wetlands are usually flat, and often have very fertile soil. This makes them good places for farming. Over the years, many of the world's wetlands have been drained and plowed up, and are now used to grow crops. Wetlands are also disappearing because we use a large amount of water in our daily lives.

AN EPIC JOURNEY

American and European eels live partly in fresh water, and partly in the sea. Eels lay their eggs in the Sargasso Sea, east of Florida. The young eels are then carried north by the ocean, and for three or four years, they feed and grow. When the eels near the shore, they change into elvers. They swim up rivers, and spend 10 years or more feeding. Eventually, they return to the Sargasso Sea to lay eggs of their own.

POND LIFE

1 Damselfly
2 Frog
3 Coot
4 Newt
5 Great diving beetle
6 Water strider
7 Back swimmer
8 Stickleback
9 Water spider
10 Water scorpion
11 Great crested grebe
12 Frog spawn
13 Frog tadpole
14 Caddis fly larva

▼ In spring and summer, a pond looks calm and inviting. But like all habitats, it is the place where animals take part in a deadly battle for survival. Water striders and back swimmers eat small animals that fall onto the surface. Frogs eat all kinds of food, from worms to beetles, while coots feed on water plants, tadpoles, snails, and even young birds. The great crested grebe eats fish and other small animals.

▲ All mammals breathe air, so they can only stay underwater for a short time. The water vole lives mainly on water plants. It raises its young in a tunnel, dug in the banks of a stream or river. Although often called the water rat, its blunt nose and furry tail show that it is a vole.

F

frog

A frog is an AMPHIBIAN with long hind legs adapted for jumping. It has thin moist skin and cannot survive in very dry places. A frog lays eggs that turn into tadpoles. Most frogs lay their eggs in ponds or pools, but some frogs carry their eggs in pouches on their backs, or in their mouths, or even their stomachs. Other frogs lay their eggs on leaves overhanging water, and make a ball of foam that keeps the eggs damp. See **reproduction**.

◀ A frog has lungs, but it is also able to breathe through its skin. During the breeding season, many frogs croak loudly.

fulmar

Fulmars are small gray-and-white seabirds that nest on rocky ledges around northern oceans. They are steadily increasing in numbers and spreading into new areas. Fulmars eat fish, and often take the waste that is thrown overboard from fishing boats.

fur seal

Fur seals are more closely related to the SEA LIONS than to true seals. They live mainly in the Pacific Ocean, and like sea lions, they have small ear flaps and can twist their hindfeet forward when walking on land. Fur seals are nearly 6 feet (2 m) long. They have a thick coat of fur all over their bodies, and several species of fur seal were once hunted close to extinction.

gannet

One of the largest seabirds in the northern hemisphere, the gannet has a wingspan of up to 6 feet (2 m). It makes spectacular dives to catch fish, plummeting from a height of 100 feet (30 m), and entering the sea with a huge splash. See **booby**.

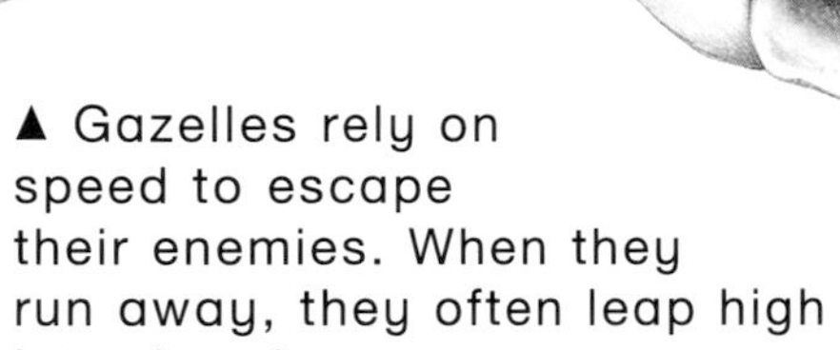

▲ Gazelles rely on speed to escape their enemies. When they run away, they often leap high into the air.

gazelle

Gazelles are small and slender grazing ANTELOPES that are found mainly in Africa. One of the commonest is Thomson's gazelle, which lives in East Africa, and forms large herds up to 500 strong. Both male and female have long, slightly curved horns, and they measure about 3 feet (1 m) from nose to tail.

G

gecko

Geckos are extraordinary nocturnal LIZARDS that can run up smooth walls, and even across ceilings, without falling off. Their feet have pads with many tiny hairs, and the pads can grip flat surfaces like suckers. Geckos hunt insects, and they have large eyes. They climb up trees and rocks, and also come into houses.

▲ Gerbils live on leaves and seeds. They often get all the water they need from their food, so they do not need to drink.

gerbil

Gerbils are small RODENTS that live in the deserts of Africa and Asia. They have large eyes and ears, and very long whiskers. Like many desert animals, gerbils are nocturnal, and they have a special way of saving water. Their long pointed noses contain many tiny passages, and these collect water from the gerbil's breath when it breathes out.

gerenuk

A gerenuk is a type of GAZELLE that has an exceptionally long, thin neck, and legs that are almost like stilts. It lives in DESERT and semi-desert areas of East Africa, where there is little or no grass. Thorn trees are the main source of food, and the gerenuk reaches the leaves by standing on its hindlegs, with its front legs propped against a tree trunk.

▶ A gibbon can grip branches with its hands and its feet. Its arms are much longer than its legs, and they can easily support its full body weight.

gibbon

When hanging from a branch, a gibbon measures about 6 feet (2 m) from its fingers to its toes. Gibbons are the smallest APES, and they spend most of their time in trees. They use their long arms to swing from branch to branch. Gibbons feed mainly on fruit and leaves, but they also eat insects and birds' eggs. They live in the tropical RAIN FORESTS of Southeast Asia.

gila monster

The gila monster is a black and yellow LIZARD, about 2 feet (60 cm) long, that is found in the southern United States and in Mexico. Its tail is full of fat. The fat helps it to survive when food is scarce. The gila monster is one of only two lizards that have a poisonous bite.

▶ The gila monster's bright colors warn that it is dangerous, and should not be attacked. It injects its poison through special grooved teeth.

G

giraffe

The giraffe is the tallest animal on four legs, and can reach 20 feet (6 m) in height. Giraffes live on the African grasslands. They have very tough mouths and tongues, and can chew up the leaves and thorns without being harmed. During the breeding season, male giraffes often wrestle with each other using their heads and necks. See **grassy plains**.

▲ With its long neck, a giraffe can reach the juiciest leaves at the top of thorn trees. It can reach higher than an elephant's trunk.

glowworm

Not a worm but a BEETLE, the glowworm is about $\frac{1}{3}$ inch (1 cm) long. After dark, the female makes a soft greenish light. This light attracts males, which come to mate with her. See **firefly**.

gnu

The gnu, or wildebeest, is not as pretty or graceful as other types of ANTELOPE. It has heavy curved horns, a dull gray coat and a fringe of whitish hair under its chin, like a beard. Gnus live in very large herds on African plains, and make long MIGRATIONS. See **grassy plains**.

goat

Wild goats are mountain MAMMALS, superbly adapted for climbing steep rock faces and living on whatever vegetation they can find. The goats kept on farms are descended from these wild animals. They are also good climbers. See **domestic animals**.

▲ Most gobies have long bodies and live in shallow water.

goby

Gobies are small fish that live mainly in salt water. They include the smallest fish in the world, the dwarf goby, which lives in lakes in the Philippines. It rarely grows to more than $\frac{1}{3}$ inch (1 cm) long.

golden eagle

Like other large BIRDS OF PREY, the golden eagle can kill animals several times its own size, but it generally feeds on fairly small animals, such as rabbits, marmots, and ground squirrels. See **eagle**.

▶ Golden eagles were once common in the mountains of Europe, Asia, and North America, but they are now rare.

goldfish
Goldfish are probably the best-known FISH in the world, because they are often kept as pets. Goldfish are a type of carp. Their wild ancestors live in the ponds and lakes of Asia and eastern Europe, and are dull brown in color.

goose
A goose is a large, sturdy waterbird with a strong beak. It feeds on water plants or grass and other plants on land. There are many different types of wild geese and most of them fly long distances to the area where they nest in summer. Most wild geese in Europe and North America breed in the far north, close to the Arctic Circle. Farmyard geese are descended from wild geese and are often white. See **birds**, **migration**, **tundra**.

◀ Pink-footed geese breed in the Arctic, but travel south during winter to warmer climates.

gorilla
Despite its reputation as a ferocious giant, the gorilla is actually a very gentle leaf-eating APE. Male gorillas can grow to 6 feet (1.8 m) tall, and weigh over 440 pounds (200 kg). Gorillas live in forests high up in the mountains of central Africa. Hunting is a major threat to gorillas. A whole family group may be killed so that the young ones can be captured and sold to zoos. See **communication**.

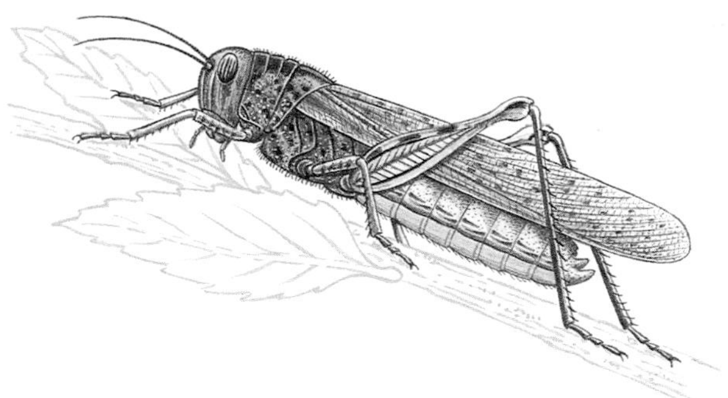

▲ Grasshoppers "sing" by rubbing their legs against their wings.

grasshopper
Grasshoppers are leaf-eating INSECTS with very long back legs. These legs are equipped with powerful muscles that allow the grasshopper to make jumps up to 3 feet (1 m) high. Most grasshoppers can fly, but they usually escape from birds and other insect-eating animals by jumping instead. See **cricket**, **locust**.

grassy plains see **pages 58 and 59**

grebe
Grebes are waterbirds that carry their chicks on their backs as they swim about. The parents even dive underwater with the chicks still "on board." Grebes feed on small fish and insect grubs. See **birds**, **fresh water**.

greenfly see **aphid**

ground squirrel
Unlike most SQUIRRELS, ground squirrels rarely climb trees. Instead, they search on the ground for nuts and seeds, or dig for plant roots. Ground squirrels have bushy tails, and their fur is often stripy. They usually live in burrows, although some make nests among piles of boulders. See **chipmunk**, **hibernation**.

GRASSY PLAINS

Large areas of the world are naturally covered by grass. They include the savannahs of East Africa, the prairies of North America, the steppes of Mongolia, and the grasslands of Australia. Grassland occurs where there is too little rainfall for forests to survive, but enough rain to prevent the land becoming a desert. Grasslands are the home of large herds of grass-eating animals such as ZEBRAS and ANTELOPES in Africa, and KANGAROOS in Australia. Grasslands are also the home of seed-eating birds, such as OSTRICHES, EMUS, and QUELEAS, which live in enormous flocks. Meadows and pastures are types of grassland that have been created by clearing forests.

AUSTRALIAN GRASSLANDS

Large parts of Australia are made up of dry grassy plains. Because it is an island, Australia has developed grassland animals that are found nowhere else. The most famous of these are the kangaroos. Several kinds of kangaroo feed on grass, including the red kangaroo, which is Australia's largest. The emu also eats grass, but it prefers fruit, seeds, and insects.

▼ African grasslands are home to large numbers of animals. They line up to drink at the water holes, especially in the evening.

THE STEPPES OF ASIA

Steppes are grassy plains without trees. The Asian steppes are the home of the saiga. Hamsters feed on plants and seeds.

GRASSLANDS IN DANGER

One of the greatest threats to grasslands is overgrazing. Where there are many cattle and goats, the plants become stunted, and the soil is exposed. If this happens, the soil can wash or blow away and the grassland may turn into a desert.

LIFE IN AN AFRICAN GRASSLAND

1 Meerkat
2 Gnu or Wildebeest
3 Zebra
4 Dung beetle
5 Marabou stork
6 Impala
7 Elephant
8 Lion
9 Ostrich
10 Weaver bird
11 Giraffe

grouse

The grouse is a plump BIRD with short legs and wings. It can fly only a short distance and it stays low to the ground, with its wings making a loud whirring noise. Grouse live on moorland, on prairies, or in forests, and feed on plants. They nest on the ground.

▶ A guillemot's egg has a very sharp point. If it is accidentally moved, it rolls around in a circle instead of falling into the sea.

guillemot

Guillemots are black or black and white seabirds that stand upright when they are out of water. They are good swimmers, but on land they walk with a slow waddle. In spring, they flock to tall sea cliffs with narrow ledges. They do not build nests, but lay their eggs on the bare rock.

◀ Young guinea pigs develop very quickly. They can live on their own when they are just five days old.

guinea pig

These South American RODENTS originally lived on rocky mountainsides, but today they are much more common as pets. Wild guinea pigs, or cavies, live in underground burrows. They feed mainly on grass and leaves.

gull see **seagull**

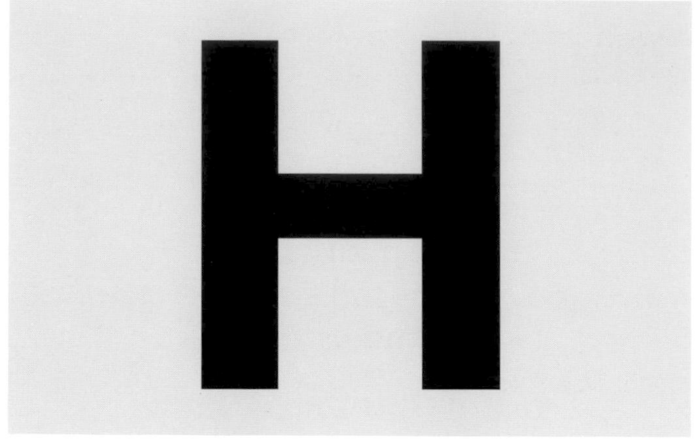

habitats see **pages 62 and 63**

haddock

The haddock is a type of FISH, similar to a COD, but slightly smaller. It lives in the North Atlantic. Haddock feed near the seabed, eating worms, mollusks and small fish. The female haddock lays her eggs in the open water. See **open seas**.

halibut

The halibut is one of the largest kinds of FLATFISH, growing up to 8 feet (2.5 m) long. Instead of spending all their time on the seabed, halibuts swim about and catch other fish. They live in deep water.

hammerhead shark

Nobody knows why this SHARK has a T-shaped head. Hammerheads feed on fish and dead animals, and they have been known to attack humans. They can measure over 20 feet (6 m).

▶ The hammerhead's eyes and nostrils are far apart. This may help it to track its food.

hamster

Wild hamsters live in grassland or semi-desert areas of Europe, the Middle East, and Asia. They are nocturnal RODENTS that eat seeds, roots, and some insects. Hamsters build up large stores for the winter months by collecting food in their cheek-pouches, and carrying it back to their burrows.

▶ The brown hare keeps its color all the year round, but the snowshoe hare turns white in winter.

hare

Hares are MAMMALS that are closely related to RABBITS, but they have bigger bodies, longer legs, and longer ears. Hares live above ground, and they give birth to their young in a hollow called a form. Hares feed mainly at night. During the day they rest among long grass.

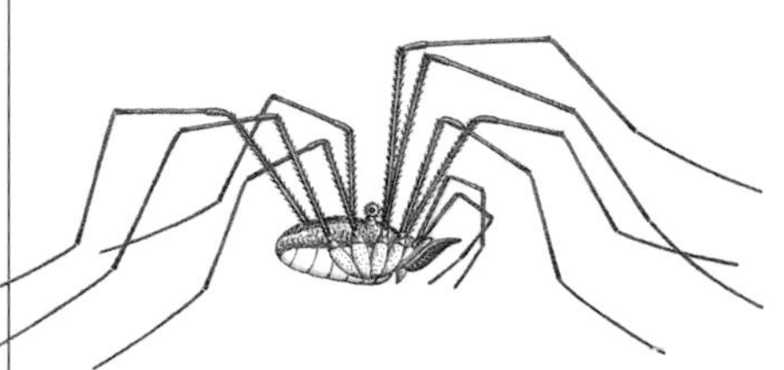

◀ Harvest-men look like spiders, but they have very slender legs. They can shed legs.

harvestman

The harvestman, or daddy longlegs, is an eight-legged animal related to the SPIDERS. Its body is generally small and pear-shaped, while the legs are very long and thin. Harvestmen hunt for small insects. See **arachnid**.

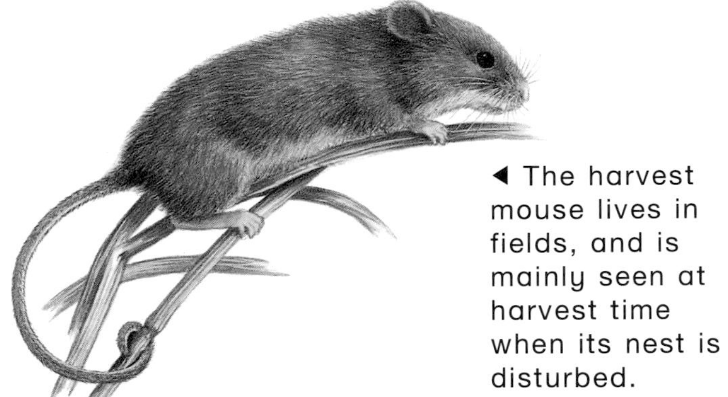

◀ The harvest mouse lives in fields, and is mainly seen at harvest time when its nest is disturbed.

harvest mouse

This tiny MOUSE makes its nest from grass blades. It weaves them into a ball about 3 inches (8 cm) across, which is held up by grass stems. The harvest mouse raises up to 12 young inside its snug home. They are found in Europe and eastern Asia.

Hawaiian goose

The Hawaiian GOOSE, or nene, was once almost extinct. By 1950, there were only 30 birds left. To try to save the species, eggs were flown to sanctuaries around the world. The rescue was a great success.

hawk

The word hawk is used for many different BIRDS OF PREY. The hawk family includes EAGLES and BUZZARDS, but many of the birds called hawks are smaller, and live by hunting birds or small mammals. See **kite**.

▶ Hawks may also eat lizards.

HABITATS

Humans can live in many places. Although we do not like too much heat or too much rain, we can cope with different climates and different surroundings without too much trouble. Most wild animals are not like this. Instead, they have evolved special ways of life, so that each kind fits into a particular habitat. For example, a polar bear is equipped to survive on ice and tundra, but it would not last for long in a desert. A kangaroo is good at surviving in dry grassland, but it would find little to eat in a coniferous forest. These different kinds of surroundings are called habitats. Each habitat has its own collection of plants and animals, and these depend on each other in the struggle to survive.

LIVING TOGETHER

Many plants and animals live closely together. Plants harness energy from the Sun, and animals either eat plants, or eat each other. In each habitat, living things often depend on one another in unexpected ways. For example, many grassland trees produce food that is eaten by ants. The ants attack anything that tries to eat the tree's leaves. Together, the tree and its ants have a better chance of survival.

▶ The South Pole is covered with ice all year round, but in the Arctic some of the ice melts in summer, uncovering the tundra.

KEY

- Polar regions
- Tundra
- Mountains
- Coniferous forest
- Deciduous forest
- Rain forests
- Desert
- Grassy plains

▼ On these two pages you can see the world's most important habitats. Tropical rain forests lie near the Equator, where the air is moist and the Sun almost overhead. Farther to the north and south, in the subtropics, the air is drier, but the sunshine is still strong. Temperate zones are still farther away from the Equator. Here, the climate is much cooler, and forests are widespread. Near the poles it is too cold for trees, but the seas are full of life.

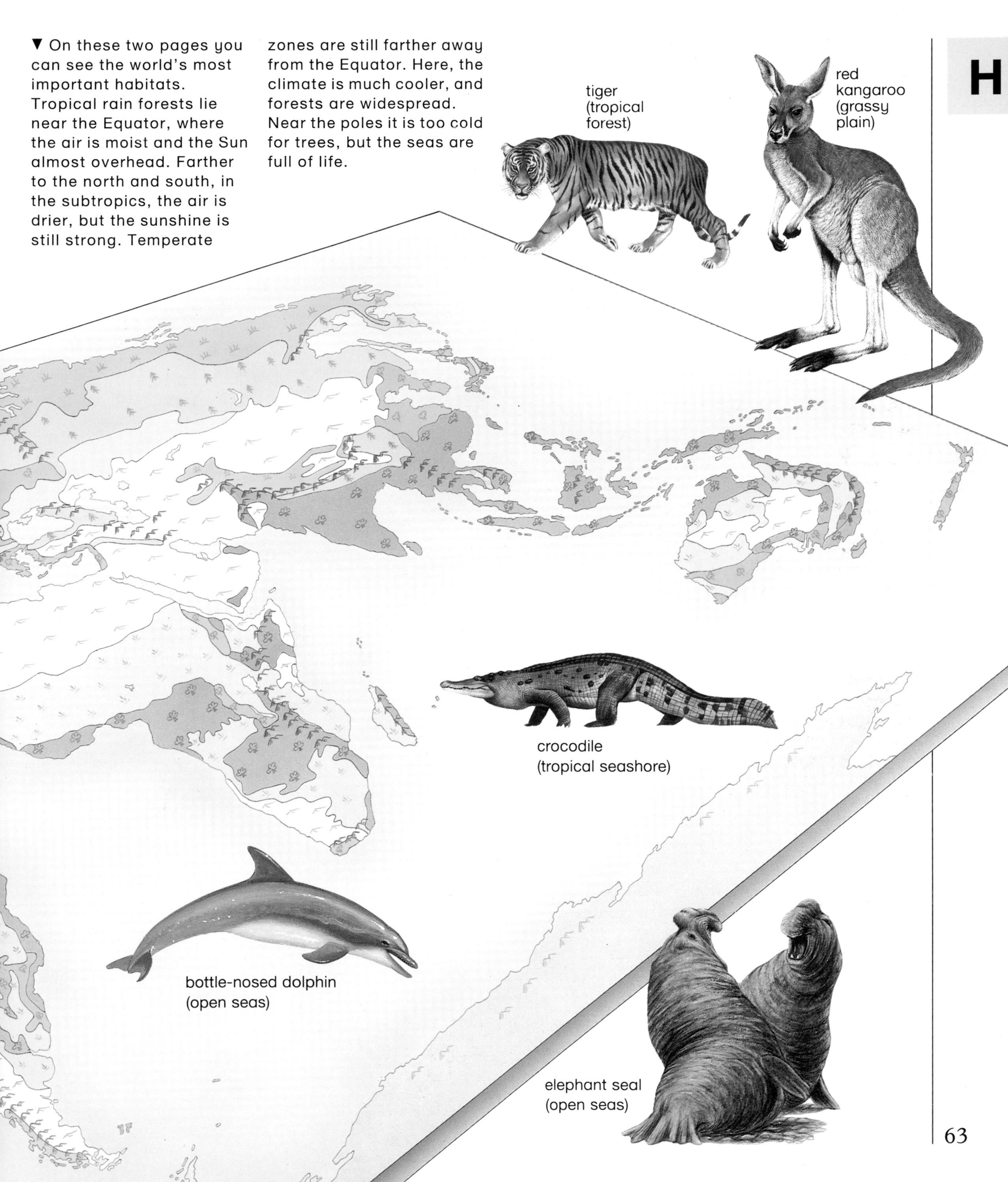

H

hawkmoth

In cool parts of the world, hawkmoths are the largest and most spectacular moths. Hawkmoths have heavy but streamlined bodies, and they fly quickly and powerfully. Most are nocturnal, but a few fly by day. Some hawkmoths hover in front of flowers and drink their nectar. Hawkmoths have large caterpillars with a sharp, curved spine on their tail end, and some are serious pests of crops. See **butterflies and moths**.

▲ The death's head hawkmoth has a skull-like marking on the back of its body. Its caterpillars often feed on potato plants.

hedgehog

When the dinosaurs still stalked the Earth, over 70 million years ago, the first hedgehogs were already living in the undergrowth and coming out after dark to feed. These MAMMALS have survived, thanks to the sharp spines on their backs, which protect them from predators. When a hedgehog is threatened, it curls up into a spiny ball, with its soft belly tucked up inside. Hedgehogs eat insects and worms. They live in Europe, Asia, and Africa, in many different habitats. Some hedgehogs live in DESERTS, while others survive well in towns. They can sometimes be heard snuffling and snorting in European backyards at night. See **defense**.

hermit crab

These unusual seashore CRABS do not have a hard covering over the hind end of their bodies. To protect themselves, they reverse into the empty shells of MOLLUSKS, and use them as their homes. A hermit crab's hind end curves to one side, so that it can fit into a spiral shell. See **animal partnerships**.

heron

Herons are long-legged BIRDS that wade into the shallows of rivers and estuaries in search of fish. They find their food by keeping very still, and then suddenly stabbing with their sharp beaks.

herring

These silvery, torpedo-shaped fish are about 12 inches (30 cm) long. They feed on fish near the surface of the sea, and they often form large schools. During the day, they sink into deeper water.

hibernation see **page 65**

hippopotamus

In the rivers and lakes of Africa, the hippopotamus wallows during the day to keep cool. Its eyes and nostrils are on top of its head, so it can see and breathe while the rest of its body is under water.

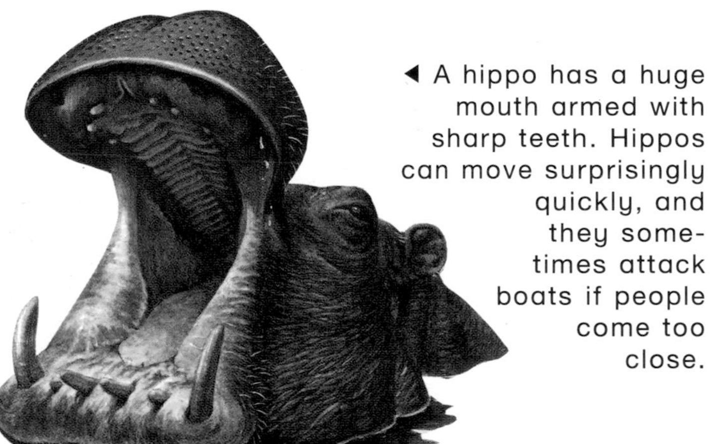

◀ A hippo has a huge mouth armed with sharp teeth. Hippos can move surprisingly quickly, and they sometimes attack boats if people come too close.

HIBERNATION

Animals that cannot find enough food in the winter months go into a state known as hibernation. A hibernating animal looks as if it is sleeping, but it usually cannot wake even if it is picked up. Animals that hibernate include HEDGEHOGS, GROUND SQUIRRELS, and some BEARS. Cold-blooded animals, such as TORTOISES and many INSECTS, may also go into a dormant state during winter, but this is not quite the same as true hibernation. In parts of the world that have hot summers or a dry season, some animals enter a special summer sleep. This is called aestivation.

▶ The poorwill of North America is the only bird known to hibernate. Hibernating poorwills are usually found in deserts, where the winter is cold.

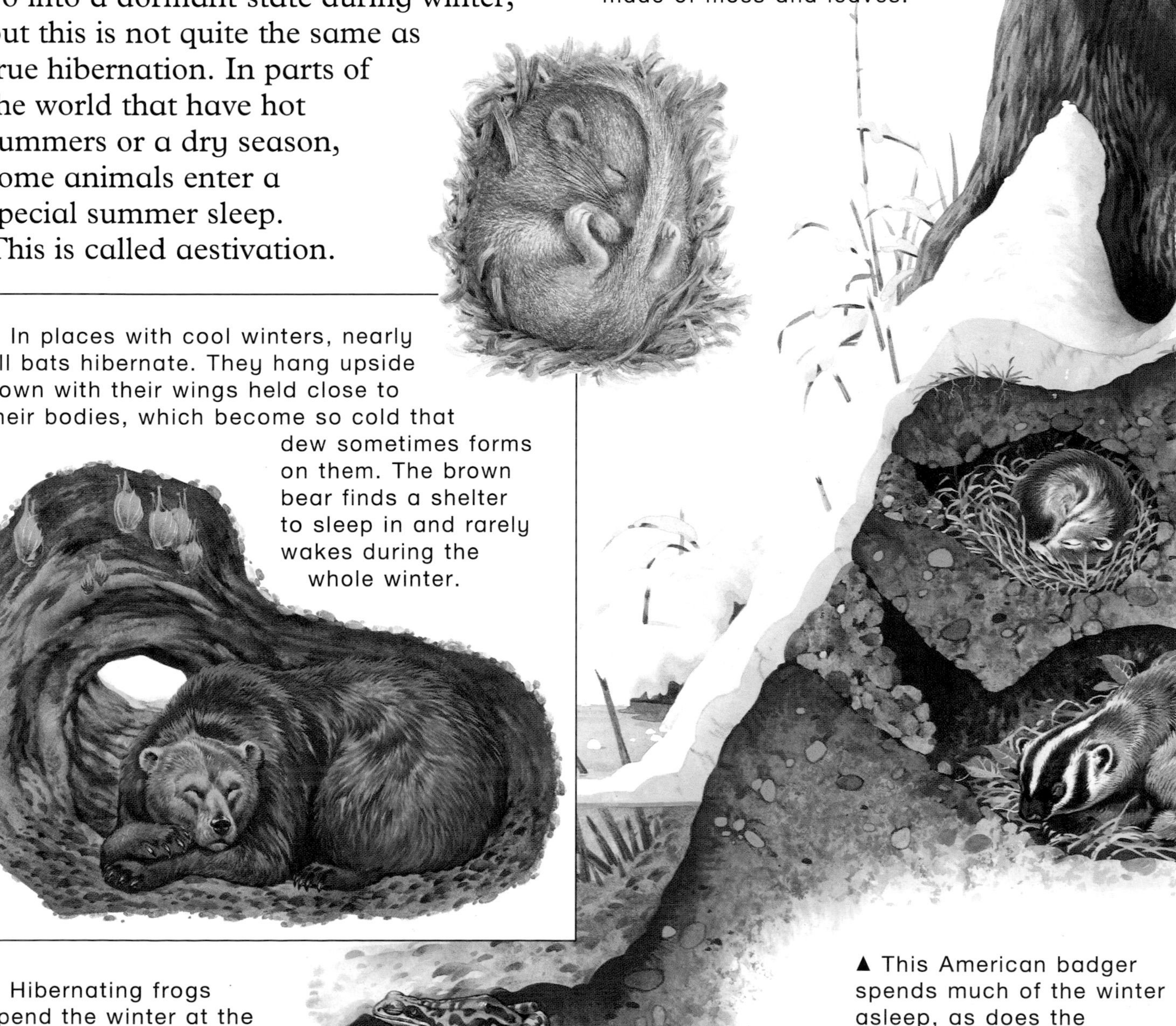

▼ The dormouse hibernates inside a special winter nest, made of moss and leaves.

▼ In places with cool winters, nearly all bats hibernate. They hang upside down with their wings held close to their bodies, which become so cold that dew sometimes forms on them. The brown bear finds a shelter to sleep in and rarely wakes during the whole winter.

▶ Hibernating frogs spend the winter at the bottom of ponds, away from the ice above.

▲ This American badger spends much of the winter asleep, as does the woodchuck, a kind of marmot.

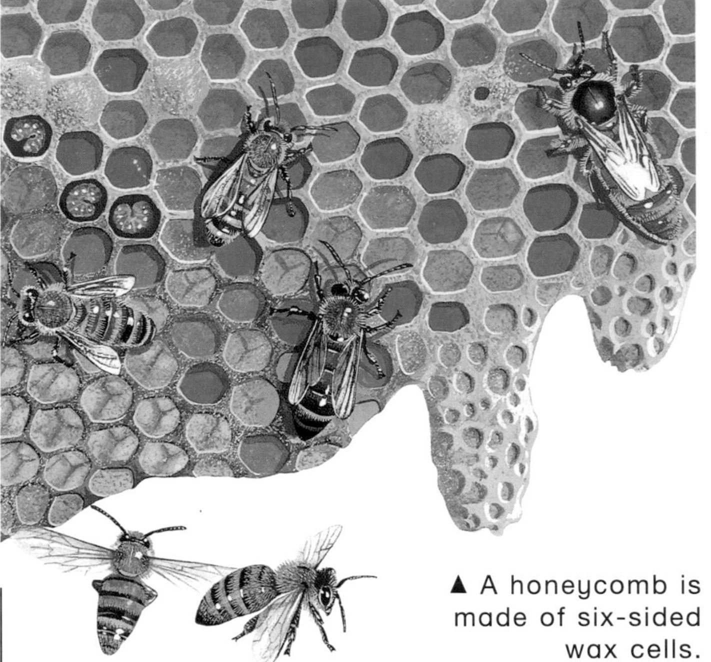

▲ A honeycomb is made of six-sided wax cells.

honeybee

These busy INSECTS collect pollen and nectar, and they use it to make honey, which is their food for the winter. Honeybees live in huge family groups, containing up to 100,000 individuals, and they make nests out of a special wax. In the wild, they build their nests in holes in trees, but people who keep honeybees give them special nest boxes, called hives. A honeybee nest contains a single queen, who lays all the eggs. Most of the other bees bring up the young, or fly off to collect food. Honeybees are found all over the world. See **bee**.

honey ant

In the nests of these strange insects, some of the ants act as living food stores. When the colony is short of food, the worker ants make the storage ants bring up or regurgitate the sweet sap they have eaten, to feed the rest of the colony.

hoofed mammals see **ungulates**

hoopoe

The hoopoe gets its name from its loud, whooping cry. This boldly colored BIRD has a crest of pinkish-orange feathers, tipped with black and white, that it can erect in a spectacular display. The hoopoe is almost 12 inches (30 cm) long. It uses its strong curved beak to probe in the ground for worms and insects.

▶ Hoopoes lay their eggs in an underground hole, or in a cavity inside a tree-trunk.

hornbill

These large-beaked BIRDS are found in the tropics of Africa and Asia. During the breeding season, the female lays her eggs in a hollow tree. The male then closes up the opening to the hollow with mud, leaving only a small slit through which he can feed his mate. This unique way of nesting protects the female hornbill and her chicks from predators.

◀ Hornbills feed on fruit and small animals, using their long and sharp beaks.

hornet

A very large WASP, the hornet is much feared because of its size, but is actually less likely to sting than many smaller wasps. Hornets do not have black stripes but are colored yellow and orangy-red. They often feed on other INSECTS.

horse

Horses are hoofed MAMMALS, or UNGULATES. They feed on grass. They have sharp front teeth to cut the grass, and wide back teeth to grind it up. The world's only true wild horses live in Central Asia. Known as Przewalski's horse, this is thought to be the ancestor of domesticated horses, and is now very rare. Other "wild" horses, such as those in the Camargue region of southern France, are descendants of horses that escaped long ago, and that roam free. See **domestic animals**.

▼ Unlike domesticated horses, Przewalski's horses have short upright manes.

horseshoe crab see **king crab**

house martin

This small insect-eating BIRD often builds its nest under the eaves of houses. It gathers mud from puddles and roadsides, and packs it together to form a cup-shaped nest. See **migration**, **swallow**.

hover fly

There are hundreds of different kinds of hover fly, and all are small harmless INSECTS that feed on nectar from flowers. They get their name from their habit of hovering in front of the flowers.

▼ Howler monkeys call to each other in the rain forests of South America.

howler monkey

Howler monkeys have a bone in the throat that is greatly enlarged and hollow like a drum. It makes their howling much louder. A troop of howler monkeys call to establish their territorial rights in a certain area of forest, and neighboring troops howl back.

hummingbird

These tiny BIRDS feed on nectar from flowers, using special beaks that are shaped like a drinking straw. Most hummingbirds hover in front of flowers, and their wings move so rapidly that they look like a blur. The bee hummingbird is the world's smallest bird.

H

humpback whale

The most elaborate songs in the animal world are not sung by a bird but by humpback whales, which call to each other for hours on end in the warm tropical seas where they breed. Humpback whales spend the winter months in the tropics, then migrate to cooler waters in the summer. The humpback's pregnancy lasts for 11 months or more, so baby humpbacks are born in tropical waters when the females return again the following year. The young are fed on milk for almost a year.

▲ Humpback whales can be 62 feet (19 m) long. They sometimes burst upward through the surface, before crashing back into the sea.

hyena

Although they look quite like dogs, hyenas are actually more closely related to CATS. Hyenas feed on the carcasses left by other predators, although they also kill some animals for themselves. They have very strong jaws, and can crunch through bones to extract the marrow inside. The largest kind, the spotted hyena, can grow to 6 feet (1.8 m) long. Hyenas live in Africa and parts of Asia, in grassland and semi-desert areas.

ibex

The ibex is a type of wild GOAT. It is about the same size as its domestic relative, but has unusually long horns. It is found in Italy, Switzerland, and in parts of the Middle East, Afghanistan, and Kashmir.

ibis

The ibis that is found in Africa was regarded as a god by the Ancient Egyptians. This wading BIRD lives mainly in marshlands, feeding on frogs, insects, and insect grubs. Other species of ibis are found around the world, all with the same downcurved beaks and bare skin on the face. Ibises generally breed in large colonies, often in the branches of mangrove trees.

▲ Ibises usually breed in large groups, and they make their nests in low trees.

ichneumon

Ichneumons are slender INSECTS, related to the bees and ants, and are found all over the world. With their long, pointed "tails," they look rather threatening, but are actually harmless and do not sting. However, they are a threat to caterpillars, because they lay their eggs inside caterpillars' bodies. When the eggs hatch, the ichneumon grubs feed on the caterpillar, which slowly dies. Some females are over 4 inches (10 cm) long.

◄ Marine iguanas can grow up to 5 feet (1.5 m) long from head to tail.

iguana

An iguana is a type of LIZARD. Iguanas are often colorful, and several kinds have spectacular courtship displays. Most iguanas are found in the Americas, but some live in Fiji and Madagascar. The most unusual are the marine iguanas of the Galapagos Islands. They are the only lizards in the world that feed in the sea.

impala

One of the most beautiful ANTELOPES, the impala has long, curved horns. It lives in grassland and open woodland in East Africa. Like the GAZELLE, to which it is related, the impala makes enormous leaps when pursued by a predator. Impalas often form very large herds of up to 200 animals. See **grassy plains**.

insects

Insects are INVERTEBRATES that have hard external skeletons and jointed legs. Counting legs is the simplest way to recognize an adult insect. They always have three pairs, although some may be quite small. Insects are a remarkably successful group of animals. They live all over the world, on land, in the air, and in freshwater, but not in the sea, and they eat all kinds of food, from plant sap to wool. Young insects often look quite different from their parents, and they change shape as they grow up. See **arthropod**, **reproduction**.

INSECTS

Insects' bodies are all built on the same plan, with a head at the front, a middle part called a thorax, and a rear part called an abdomen. Simple insects, such as the silverfish, do not have wings, and hardly change shape as they grow up.

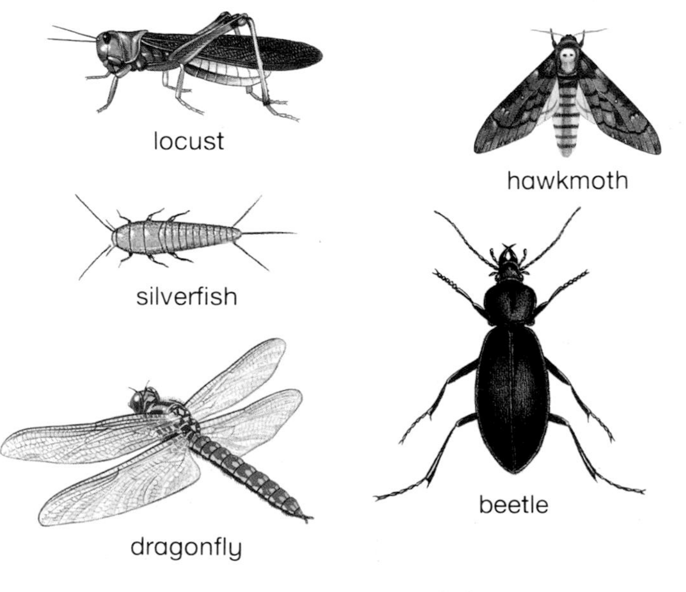

I

invertebrates

Scientists divide animals into two major groups—those with a backbone and those without. All those with a backbone, called VERTEBRATES, are quite closely related to each other. Those without a backbone, the invertebrates, are much more varied. They include the ARTHROPODS, such as insects, spiders, and crustaceans, the MOLLUSKS, such as snails, slugs, and squids, and also WORMS, STARFISH, JELLYFISH, and a great variety of other animals. Invertebrates make up most of the animals on Earth. The largest are several feet long, but the smallest can only be seen with a microscope.

INVERTEBRATES

Over nine-tenths of the animal species on Earth are invertebrates. Most invertebrates are small, soft-bodied animals, but some have hard cases or shells. The giant squid can grow to over 50 feet (15 m) long, and is the largest invertebrate.

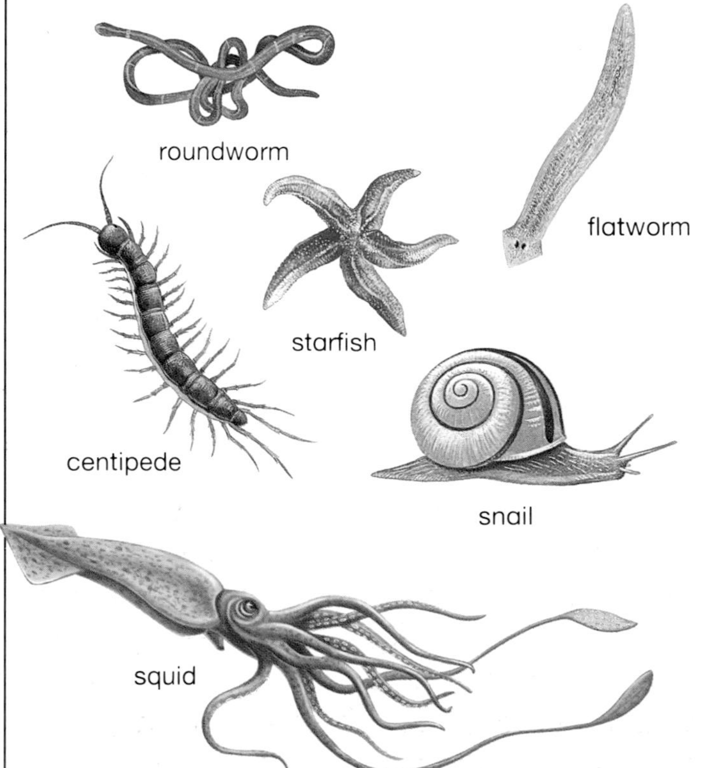

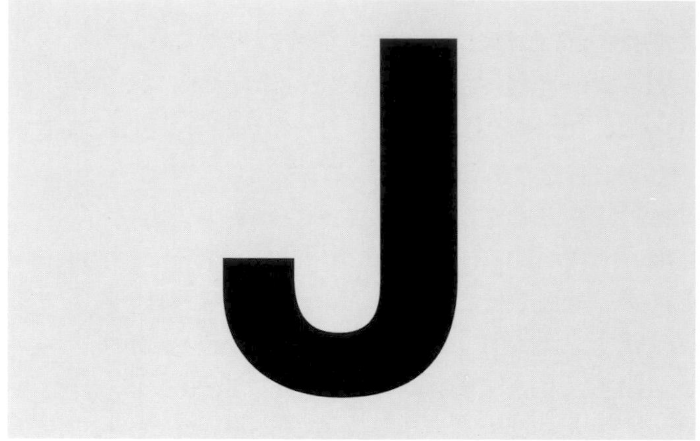

jackal

Jackals are close relatives of DOGS and WOLVES, although they are lightly built, and look more like FOXES. They are found mainly in Africa, although one species, the golden jackal, lives in the Middle East and in India.

jackdaw

The jackdaw is a member of the CROW family. It is smaller than other crows, and has neat, glossy black plumage and a gray head. Jackdaws are found mainly in Europe. They often nest on buildings, and usually feed in fields.

▶ Most jaguars have yellow and brown spotted fur, but some are almost black.

jaguar

In the forests and grasslands of South America, the jaguar is the most powerful predator. This large member of the CAT family feeds mainly on piglike animals called peccaries, and also on large rodents called capybaras. Jaguars have beautiful spotted fur, and have suffered a great deal through hunting.

jay

Although they are members of the CROW family, jays are not black like other crows. Many are brightly colored. Jays are found in Europe, Asia, and North America. They feed on the eggs and young of other birds, together with berries, seeds, nuts, and insects.

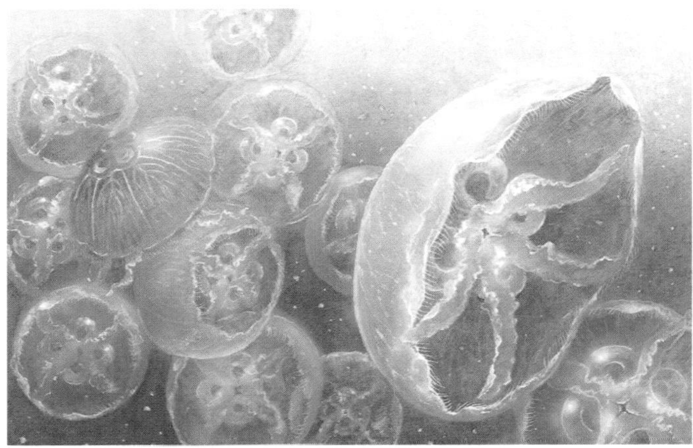

▲ Jellyfish swim jerkily by pumping water in and out of their bodies. Many have painful stingers on their tentacles and use them to catch food.

jellyfish

Jellyfish are COELENTERATES. They feed on other animals, paralyzing them with tiny stinging threads. Jellyfish can move, but they usually drift with the current. See **Portuguese man-of-war**.

jerboa

Jerboas are small desert RODENTS that hop on their long hind legs. They eat seeds and insects, and emerge from burrows after dark to feed. Jerboas have very large eyes and sensitive hearing. Several kinds of jerboa live in North Africa and Asia.

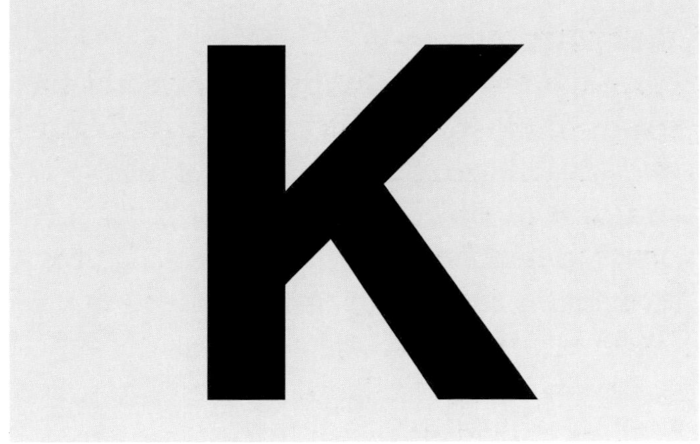

kangaroo

Kangaroos can leap as high as 10 feet (3 m), and can cover 40 feet (12 m) in a single bound. Kangaroos are the largest pouched mammals, or MARSUPIALS. They use their back legs for jumping, and their long tails to balance. The largest kangaroo is the red kangaroo, which can be about 8 feet (2.5 m) from nose to tail. Most kangaroos live in Australia and feed on grass. See **wallaby**.

▶ A young kangaroo is called a joey. If anything alarms it, a joey quickly jumps back into its mother's pouch.

kestrel

The kestrel is a small BIRD OF PREY, found in Europe, Africa, and Asia. Kestrels often hunt near highways, where there are many mice and voles in the grassy verges. By hovering in the air, they can keep a watch on the ground below, and they dive rapidly when they spot their prey.

killer whale

Killer whales have long, sharp teeth, but despite their name, they rarely threaten people. These fast black-and-white whales feed on fish, squid, sea lions, and sometimes on other whales, but they have never been known to attack humans. Killer whales are close relatives of DOLPHINS, but are much bigger. They are intelligent and playful, and they are sometimes kept in captivity. Killer whales are found worldwide, but most frequently where the sea is cool.
See **whale**.

▲ An adult killer whale can be almost 30 feet (10 m) long. It has a long upright fin on its back, which can be 7 feet (2 m) high.

king crab

Also known as horseshoe crabs, king crabs are primitive ARTHROPODS. A king crab has a hard helmet-like shell which covers the front of its body, and a long stiff tail. King crab is also the name of a large crab that lives in the northern Pacific Ocean.

kingfisher

Kingfishers are small BIRDS that often have brilliantly colored feathers and short tails. They are found all over the world. Many live by FRESH WATER, and they catch fish by diving into the water headfirst, and seizing their prey with their strong beaks. A kingfisher usually perches on a branch overhanging the water, watching for food. Some kingfishers live in forests or in grasslands and they eat large insects and small reptiles. See **kookaburra**.

▼ A kingfisher knocks its catch against a branch before swallowing it.

kite

Like HAWK, the name kite is used for several small or medium-sized BIRDS OF PREY that do not form a family or group. The Everglade kite feeds only on water snails, an unusual diet for a bird of prey.

kiwi

This flightless BIRD, found only in New Zealand, is about the size of a domestic chicken. It has a long beak and tiny wings that are completely hidden beneath its thick plumage. It has nostrils at the end of its beak, and it can find worms and insects by smell.

▲ Kiwis feed at night. Their feathers are coarse and stringy, and look like hair.

koala

This small MARSUPIAL lives in Australia, and feeds entirely on the leaves of eucalyptus trees (gum trees). Koalas are not quite as cuddly and lovable as they appear. If disturbed, they can give a painful bite. They also carry a serious disease which can be passed on to humans.

▼ The koala is one of the few animals that feed on the oily leaves of eucalyptus trees. It lives alone or in a small group.

Komodo dragon

The world's largest living LIZARD, the Komodo dragon can grow to 10 feet (3 m) in length. It is named after the island in Southeast Asia where it lives. These giant lizards feed on large animals. Only about a thousand are still alive today.

kookaburra

This brown and white Australian bird is a type of KINGFISHER that feeds on almost anything. The kookaburra swoops down on snakes, seizes them just behind the head, then flies back to its perch. It kills large ones by dropping them to the ground several times. The kookaburra is a noisy bird with a weird laughing cry.

lacewing

Lacewings are INSECTS that have large, delicate wings. Many of them have bright green bodies, and their metallic eyes reflect the light when they fly to windowpanes at night. Young lacewings feed on other insects, including aphids, midges, and mosquitoes. A lacewing larva may camouflage itself by heaping the bodies of its prey on its back. Lacewings live in all but the coldest regions of the world.

ladybug

Ladybugs are small BEETLES. There are many types of ladybugs, and they have different patterns of spots. Some have black spots on a red background, but others have red spots on black, or black spots on yellow or orange. Ladybugs are useful in the garden because they eat APHIDS (greenfly and blackfly). Young ladybugs, or larvae, are grublike, and they eat aphids as well. Ladybugs are found all over the world.

▶ A ladybug's bright colors tell birds that it tastes unpleasant.

L

leafcutter bee

Small circular holes in the leaves of garden roses are a sign that leafcutter bees live nearby. The female bee chews out the neat circles, takes them back to her nest, and rolls them into a tube. She then fills the tube with honey and pollen, and lays a single egg inside. See **bee**.

leaf insect

Leaf insects are masters of disguise. Their wings are so perfectly leaflike that they look just like the surrounding vegetation. Leaf insects are close relatives of STICK INSECTS, and most live in the tropics and subtropics. See **camouflage**.

leech

Leeches live in water and are related to EARTHWORMS, but have a sucker at each end of their bodies. A leech uses its suckers to fasten itself to an animal while it feeds on its blood. See **parasite**.

▼ In winter, the lemming makes tunnels under the snow, and searches for food.

lemming

Lemmings are small RODENTS that inhabit the cold TUNDRA regions of the Arctic. They look like small guinea pigs and they feed on plants. If food becomes short, thousands of lemmings may suddenly leave their homes, and move across country looking for somewhere else to live.

▼ When ring-tailed lemurs walk on the ground, they keep their tails high in the air.

lemur

Lemurs are related to the MONKEYS and APES, but they have pointed snouts and long bushy tails. They are found only in Madagascar. Lemurs live mainly in the trees and are very good at climbing and jumping. Most lemurs are active during the day, and they feed on fruits, insects, and birds' eggs. See **primate**.

leopard

The leopard, a large spotted CAT, lives in Africa and many parts of Asia. It can survive on the GRASSY PLAINS, high in the MOUNTAINS, in forests, or even in DESERTS. Leopards normally live on their own, and they hunt animals such as antelopes, young baboons, snakes, birds, and occasionally fish. See **snow leopard**.

▼ An adult leopard can be 10 feet (3 m) from nose to tail. It can drag an antelope's body into a tree.

lily-trotter (jacana)

The lily-trotter, or jacana, is a bird with enormously long toes. Thanks to its huge feet, it can almost "walk on water." Lily-trotters live on and around lakes in Africa, South America, Asia, and northern Australia. They run across the leaves of waterlilies and other floating waterplants.

▼ The lily-trotter's immensely long toes spread its weight, so that it does not sink when it walks across floating plants.

limpet

A limpet is a MOLLUSK that lives on rocky shores. With its stout conical shell and suckerlike foot, it can withstand the battering of powerful waves. At low tide, a limpet keeps its shell clamped to the rock. At high tide, it loosens its grip, and moves about underwater over the surface of the rock, scraping off tiny plants with its rough tongue.

lion

Although lions are sometimes called the "king of beasts," male lions are among the laziest animals on Earth. They sleep or rest for up to 20 hours a day, leaving the female lions to do most of the hunting. A group of lionesses will often hunt together, some lying in wait while the others drive the prey toward them. Lionesses working together can even kill giraffes. A group of lions is known as a pride. A pride consists of between one and three adult males, and up to 15 lionesses and their cubs. Lions are part of the CAT family, and are found mainly in Africa. See **grassy plains**.

lizard

Most lizards are fast-moving, four-legged hunters that feed on insects and other small animals. Like all REPTILES they are cold-blooded, which means that they rely on the warmth of the sun. Lizards must bask in the sun to warm themselves up in the morning. See **chameleon**, **gecko**, **iguana**, **Komodo dragon**.

▼ Many lizards can shed their tails if something catches them. They soon grow a new one.

llama

Llamas are long-necked MAMMALS from South America that are related to CAMELS. They are DOMESTICATED ANIMALS, and are kept mainly for their wool and for carrying heavy loads along steep mountain trails.

lobster

Lobsters are large CRUSTACEANS that have powerful claws. They live all over the world on the seabed in shallow water, and they use their claws to defend themselves and to catch mussels, starfish and other small animals. An adult lobster's two claws are often different in size.

▼ A lobster walks quite slowly, but it can quickly swim backward by flicking its tail.

locust

Locusts are large GRASSHOPPERS that live in the tropics. They are powerful fliers, and they sometimes form large groups or swarms and travel long distances in search of food. A swarm can contain billions of locusts. When the locusts settle, they can strip and eat every leaf from every plant, so they can have a devastating effect on farm crops.

longhorn beetle

All INSECTS have antennae, or feelers, on their heads. The antennae of a longhorn beetle can be longer than the rest of its body. Adult longhorn beetles feed on flowers, and mainly eat pollen. They lay their eggs on trees.

▲ A loris uses its large, forward-pointing eyes to find its way in the dark.

loris

Two small PRIMATES are known as lorises: the slow loris and the slender loris. Both have large staring eyes and move slowly through the trees, gripping branches. Lorises are nocturnal and live in different parts of Asia. Both eat insects, small birds, eggs, and some leaves.

louse

A louse is a small parasitic insect. Its legs are equipped with claws for clinging to skin, feathers, or fur. Sucking lice feed on blood and are found only on MAMMALS. Others, known as biting lice, live mainly on birds. See **parasite**.

▶ Male and female lovebirds often perch side-by-side to preen each other.

lovebird

These colorful birds belong to the PARROT family. Compared to most parrots they are quite small, and measure only about 6 inches (15 cm) from head to tail. They eat berries and seeds, and often feed together in noisy flocks.

lungfish

These unusual FISH have gills, but they also have lungs, and they can breathe air by taking large gulps of it at the surface. Being able to breathe air allows lungfish to live in swampy stagnant water where there is little oxygen. Most lungfish also survive periods of drought by digging a burrow in the mud and curling up inside it. Inside its burrow, a lungfish goes into a state similar to HIBERNATION.

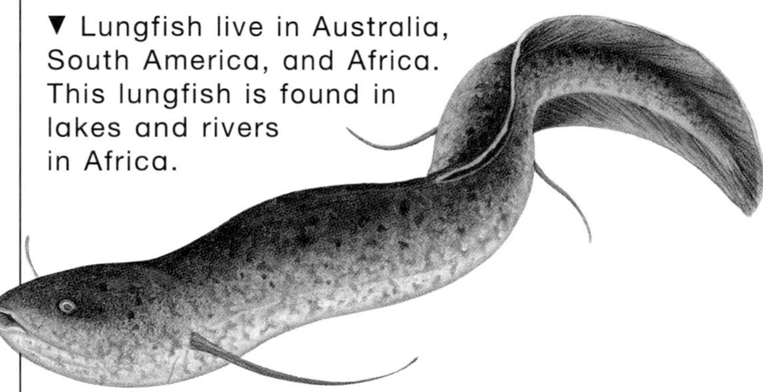

▼ Lungfish live in Australia, South America, and Africa. This lungfish is found in lakes and rivers in Africa.

lynx

The lynx is a medium-sized wild CAT with long tufted ears. Unlike most cats its tail is little more than a stump. Lynxes mainly live in coniferous forests in upland areas. They survive only in the wilder parts of Europe but are more common in Scandinavia, Asia, Canada, and Alaska.

lyrebird

These unique Australian BIRDS are dull grayish-brown in color but the males have extraordinary and spectacular tails. During his courtship display, a male bird flips his central tail feathers forward. There are two species of lyrebird. Only one, the superb lyrebird, has two outer tail feathers that are curved and form a shape like a lyre (a kind of musical instrument). Lyrebirds live mainly on the ground and feed on insects.

macaw

Macaws are large PARROTS from Central and South America that have brilliantly colored feathers and very long tails. They have powerful beaks, and feed mainly on fruit, nuts, and seeds. Macaws live in forests and open woodland. Sadly, wild macaws are becoming quite rare. This is because many have been taken captive to be sold as pets, and because the RAIN FOREST, their home, is being cut down.

▶ Like other parrots, macaws can pick up their food with their feet.

mackerel

Mackerel are fast, sleek FISH that live in large shoals in the sea. They feed on shrimps, prawns, and small fish, and grow up to 2 feet (65 cm) long. In summer, a female mackerel can produce over 400,000 eggs. Most of these are eaten by other animals, and very few of the eggs develop into adults.

▼ Magpies eat seeds and insects, but they particularly like the eggs of other birds.

magpie

Magpies are members of the CROW family, but they are more brightly colored than most of their relatives, and have very long tails. The common magpie of Europe, Asia, and western North America has distinctive black and white markings with metallic green tail feathers. It eats many kinds of food. Another kind of magpie, the azure-winged magpie, is found in Spain and the Far East. See **jay**.

mallee fowl

This turkey-sized Australian BIRD has an extraordinary way of hatching its eggs. The male builds a huge nest of rotting plant matter covered by sand. The rotting process generates heat, just like a compost heap, and the female lays her eggs in holes in the heap. As the chicks hatch, they haul themselves to the surface. Mallee fowls eat berries and insects.

mamba

The black mamba is one of the most feared SNAKES in Africa. It can be over 13 feet (4 m) long, and is slender and fast-moving. Despite its name the black mamba is actually dark gray. There are three other mambas, all green in color, which live in forest and scrub, also in Africa. All mambas feed on rodents and other small mammals, reptiles and birds.

mammal

We are mammals and so are all animals that have true hair or fur, such as DOGS, CATS, MICE, and BATS. Some mammals, including the WHALES, ELEPHANTS, and HIPPOPOTAMUSES, have lost nearly all of their hair, while in mammals such as ARMADILLOS and PANGOLINS, the hair is partly replaced by bony armor. The other important characteristic of mammals is that they feed their young on milk, produced from nipples on the underside of the female. Most mammals also give birth to live young, but monotremes do not. These egg-laying mammals are "living fossils," because they represent the link between REPTILES and mammals. See **marsupial**.

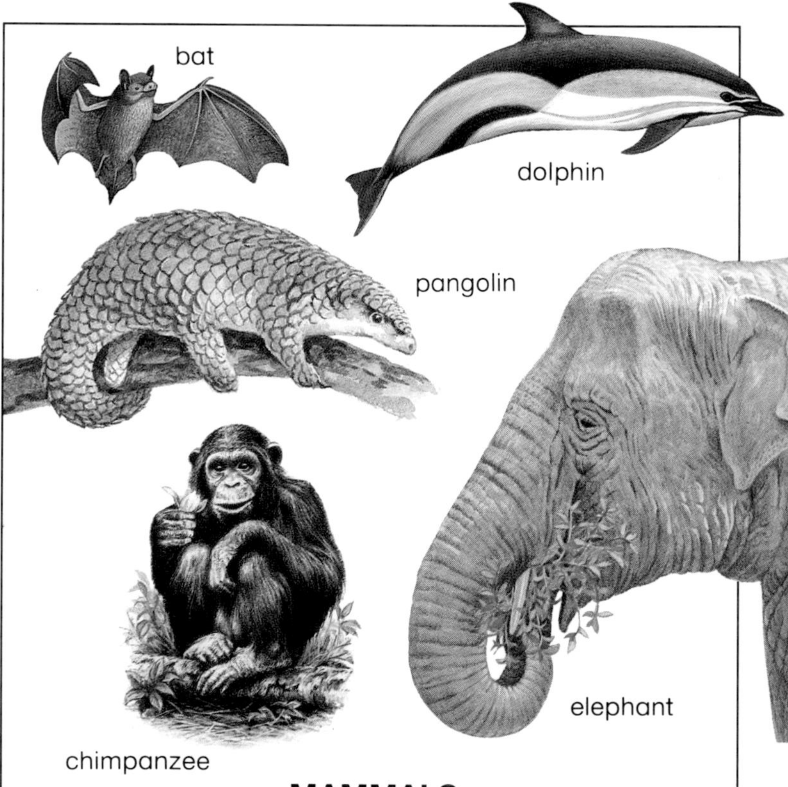

MAMMALS

Mammals live in the air, on land, and in the sea. Land mammals have legs, but many sea mammals have streamlined bodies with short flippers. A bat's front legs make up its wings.

M

mandrill

The brightly colored face of the male mandrill distinguishes it from all other MONKEYS, apart from its close relative called the drill. These two species live in the forests of West Africa and are similar to the BABOONS of the African savannahs.

man-made habitats see **pages 80 and 81**

marabou stork

The marabou stork has a bald, pinkish-red head which it often holds hunched against its body. Marabous stand over 5 feet (1.5 m) tall, and have a wingspan of over 10 feet (3 m). They are found mainly in tropical Africa. Unlike other STORKS, marabous often live far from water, and use their large beaks to pull meat from carcasses. See **grassy plains.**

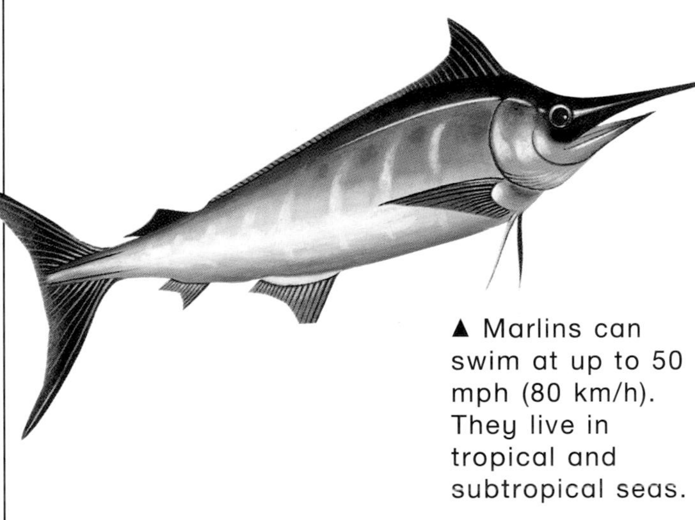

▲ Marlins can swim at up to 50 mph (80 km/h). They live in tropical and subtropical seas.

marlin

One of the world's fastest FISH, the marlin has a very long pointed "snout" which it probably uses to stun its prey. Marlins feed by swimming through schools of fish at high speed. The striped marlin grows to 10 feet (3 m), and the larger blue marlin, can reach 15 feet (4.5 m) or more.

▶ Marmosets scuttle along branches, and use their long tails for balance.

marmoset

Marmosets, together with their close relatives the tamarins, are the smallest of the MONKEYS. The tiniest of all, the pygmy marmoset, grows to only 6 inches (16 cm) long, although its tail is the same length again. Marmosets eat small birds and their eggs, fruit, leaves, insects, and spiders. Some also chew holes in the bark of trees and feed on the sugary sap that oozes out. Marmosets are found in South America and many are endangered by the destruction of forests there. They are sometimes captured and sold as pets.

marmot

These small ground-living RODENTS are related to the SQUIRRELS. They feed on seeds, roots, and other plant foods, and in the winter they hibernate, for up to six months. See **prairie dog**.

▶ Marmots stand on their back legs to look for danger. They run to their burrows if alarmed.

M

MAN-MADE HABITATS

People often talk about animals that live "in the wild." But because there are so many people on Earth, truly wild places are now becoming quite rare. Most of the habitats that we see have either been made by humans, or altered by us, and animals have had to adapt to these changes. Some animals thrive in towns and cities. Away from towns, different man-made habitats have their own wildlife. Farm crops often attract unwanted visitors, from tiny APHIDS and WEEVILS to ROOKS and DEER. Roadsides often provide a breeding ground for BUTTERFLIES, and canals and reservoirs make homes for water-birds.

◀ Ducks, herons, and gulls often feed on reservoirs and canals, and some waterbirds also breed on them. Reservoirs can be good places to spot waterbirds on migration. They often use reservoirs as "refueling" stops before continuing on their journeys.

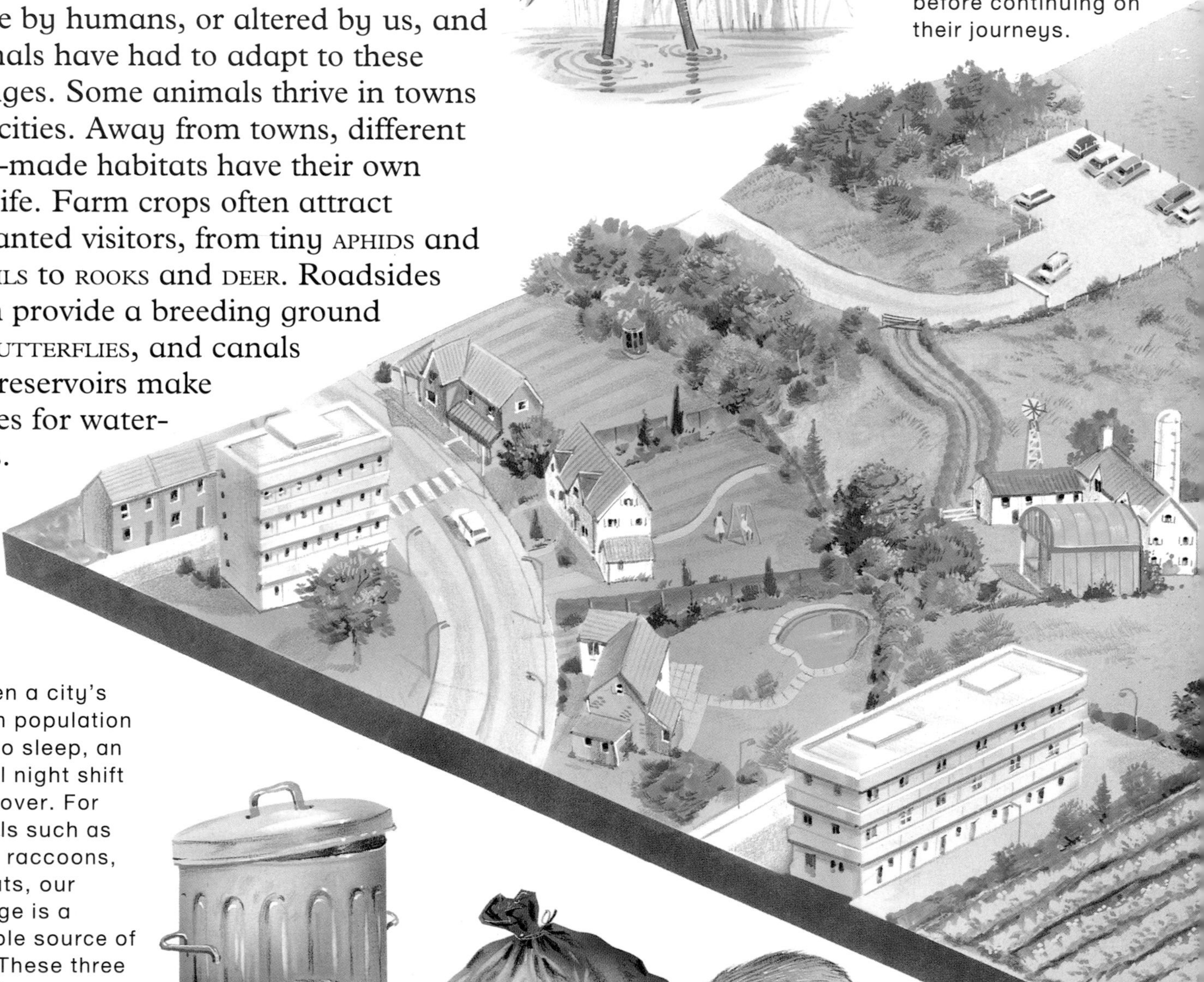

▶ When a city's human population goes to sleep, an animal night shift takes over. For animals such as foxes, raccoons, and rats, our garbage is a valuable source of food. These three animals are omnivores, which means that they can eat food of all kinds.

▶ A heathland is made up of an open patchwork of low plants and shrubs. Heathlands form when trees growing on poor soil are cut down. Heathlands are good places to see butterflies, and also birds such as warblers and grouse. After dark, bats and nightjars hunt insects.

◀ Fields are very unnatural habitats, because they often contain just one type of plant. For many animals, including insects, birds, and rodents, these crop plants are an irresistible source of food. In some countries, hedgerows around fields are important refuges for many wild plants and animals.

M

marsupials

This group of MAMMALS is found mainly in Australia, and includes KANGAROOS, WALLABIES, KOALAS, POSSUMS, and WOMBATS. There are also marsupials in New Guinea, and a few—OPOSSUMS—in South and North America. Marsupials all give birth to very tiny young. A newly-born marsupial crawls through its mother's fur and into her pouch, where it feeds on milk. When it is large enough it can leave the pouch, but it quickly returns if danger threatens. Mammals without pouches replaced the marsupials in most parts of the world many millions of years ago, for reasons that scientists do not understand.

MARSUPIALS

Marsupials are animals that have pouches. Most marsupials have pouches that face forward, but wombats and koalas have pouches that open backward. A young marsupial stays in the pouch for several weeks or months. When it leaves the pouch, it often clings to its mother.

▲ Martens are very good climbers. They can chase squirrels from branch to branch.

marten

Martens are agile cat-sized MAMMALS with long bushy tails and very short legs. They are related to the WEASELS, STOATS, and FERRETS. Martens mostly prey on small mammals such as squirrels and other rodents, but some also eat fruit and nuts.

mayfly

Mayflies are medium-sized INSECTS with large transparent wings, and three long "tails." They are dull green or brown, and are usually seen fluttering over water. Adult mayflies live no more than four days. The young mayflies develop underwater, and take up to four years to develop into adults.

midwife toad

Found only in western Europe, the midwife toad has an unusual way of caring for its eggs. As the female lays her long strings of eggs, the male toad wraps them around his hind legs. He then carries them until they hatch. When the tadpoles are about to emerge, the male goes to a pond so that the tadpoles can swim off into the water. See **toad**.

MIGRATION

In cool parts of the world, there is often a lot of food in summer, but very little in winter. Some animals make use of this summer food, but spend the winter in warmer places far away. Their long journeys are called migrations. The ARCTIC TERN probably has the longest migration of all animals, although many other birds also migrate thousands of miles each year.

All sorts of different animals carry out migrations, from WHALES and ANTELOPE to EELS and BUTTERFLIES. Some migrating animals find their way by following the coastline, or by watching the position of the sun or the stars.

◀ Swallows feed on insects. In cool places, most insects disappear during the fall, so swallows have to spend the winter somewhere else. Birds such as the bullfinch, which lives on buds and berries, have a year-round food supply. They do not need to migrate.

◀ Every year, the Arctic tern travels from the far north to the far south and then back again—a journey of more than 20,000 miles (32,000 km).

◀ Seals migrate long distances across the sea to rocky islands where they mate and have their pups.

▲ Gnus, or wildebeest, migrate to find fresh grass. They time their journeys so that they arrive just after the rains, when the grass is growing strongly.

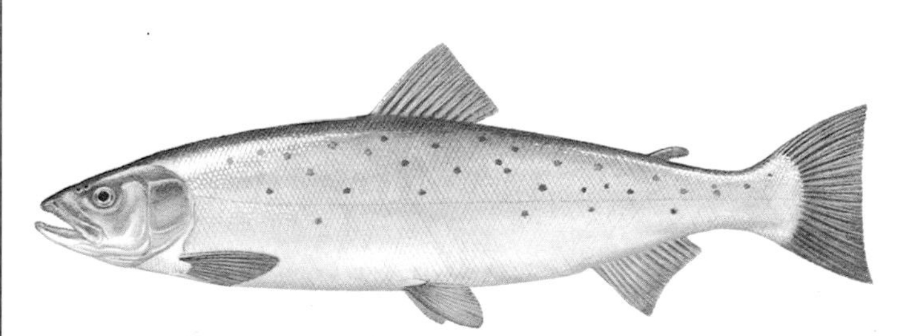

▲ Most adult salmon live in the sea, but they migrate up rivers and streams to breed. Some salmon do this just once, but others migrate every year.

millipede

Millipedes are invertebrates. They have long bodies that are carried along by dozens of tiny legs. Unlike centipedes they have two legs on each body segment. Most millipedes feed on fungi or dead leaves. Millipedes are found throughout the world and some of the tropical species are very large, with bodies as thick as a person's finger.

▶ In some parts of the world, mink are farmed for fur.

mink

Mink are small aggressive mammals related to stoats and otters. They eat a wide range of animals, including fish, crustaceans, waterbirds, and rodents, and they store food in their dens. Like some foxes, mink sometimes kill more than they need, which makes them a threat to other wildlife. Mink are native to North America and parts of Europe.

mockingbird

The dull-colored mockingbird gets its name because it often imitates the songs of other birds. It is found throughout the southern regions of North America, in gardens as well as woodlands and deserts.

▶ The mockingbird eats beetles, spiders, and other small invertebrates.

▶ Moles dig long burrows, and catch any earthworms that fall in. They also eat beetles and other small creatures.

mole

Moles are small mammals that are beautifully adapted for underground life. They have spadelike front paws for efficient burrowing, and a velvety coat that sheds the soil. Their eyes are tiny, and a mole can do little more than distinguish light from dark. All moles have very sensitive noses for feeling their way and finding prey. One species, the star-nosed mole, has a ring of fleshy pink tentacles around the tip of its nose to make it even more sensitive.

▲ The mole-rat got its name because its way of life is so like a mole. Its eyes have virtually disappeared and it has large front teeth.

mole-rat

Mole-rats are burrowing mammals that dig with their very large front teeth, rather than with their paws. Most mole-rats can close the part of their mouth behind their front teeth, so that they can burrow without swallowing soil. Mole-rats live in the drier parts of Africa and in the Middle East. They are all rodents but they belong to several families that are not closely related. Like other rodents they eat plant food, mainly roots and tubers.

mollusks

Mollusks are among the most successful of all invertebrates, and are found in many different habitats, except places that are very dry or cold. They originated in the sea, and most of them, including limpets, clams, cockles, and squid, still live in sea water. Some mollusks, particularly snails, are found in fresh water, while snails and slugs have taken up life on land. Mollusks all have soft muscular bodies, but most of them are protected by a hard shell. In some mollusks, called gastropods, the shell is coiled, while in others, called bivalves, it has two parts that hinge together. Some mollusks filter tiny food particles out of water, while others scrape away at plants, or even hunt other animals.

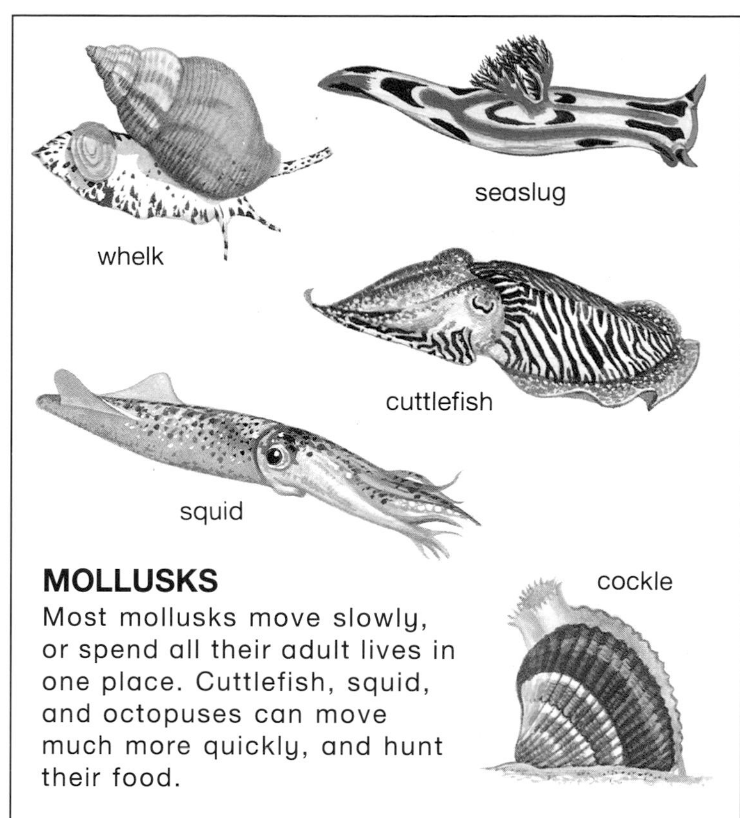

MOLLUSKS
Most mollusks move slowly, or spend all their adult lives in one place. Cuttlefish, squid, and octopuses can move much more quickly, and hunt their food.

◀ North American monarchs pack together tightly on trees and rocks in winter.

monarch

The monarch is a large and beautiful butterfly whose wings are boldly marked in black and orange. It is found in North and South America. Monarchs are powerful fliers, and in the fall many monarchs migrate from as far north as Canada to Mexico. See **migration**.

mongoose

These small hunting mammals have long slender bodies and most have very short legs. They live only in the warmer parts of the world, mainly in Africa and Asia. Mongooses eat many kinds of animals, from crabs, fish, and frogs to rodents, scorpions, and insects, but they are also fearless enemies of snakes. A mongoose will attack a snake until the snake is exhausted and cannot fight back.

▼ A mongoose avoids a cobra's deadly bite by darting out of the way if the snake strikes.

M

monitor

These large LIZARDS are hunters that attack a wide variety of other animals. The largest species, the KOMODO DRAGON, can take animals the size of deer and wild pigs. Other monitors feed on birds, snakes, other lizards, frogs, and small mammals. Monitors live in Africa, India, Southeast Asia, and Australia. Unlike most other lizards, they can stand on their hind legs.

monkey

Monkeys make up the most successful group of PRIMATES alive today. Some monkeys live in forests. Others live in open country, but they often climb trees if danger threatens. All monkeys have forward-pointing eyes and hands that can grip. Monkeys living in South America have tails that can wrap around branches. But monkeys living in Africa and Asia cannot do this. See **ape**.

▶ Some monkeys live almost entirely on leaves, but many others eat small animals, eggs, and fruit.

▶ Unlike other deer, moose spend most of the year on their own. They come together only to breed.

moose

The moose is the largest of all DEER, with a body nearly 10 feet (3 m) long and huge hand-shaped antlers. It lives in the cold northern parts of North America, and in Scandinavia and Siberia. Moose stay in forested areas, often near lakes, and in summer they wade into the water and feed on water plants.

▶ A female mosquito has piercing mouthparts. She pushes them into skin and sucks up blood. In some countries mosquitoes spread malaria.

mosquito

These small biting INSECTS are found all around the world wherever there is fresh water. Mosquitoes lay their eggs on the surface of ponds, lakes, and ditches. Female mosquitoes feed on blood from mammals or birds, causing an itchy swelling where they penetrate the skin. Male mosquitoes feed on nectar.

mountain lion see **puma**

mountains see **pages 88 and 89**

mouflon see **sheep**

▶ Mice have many enemies, but they can breed very quickly, so their numbers soon recover. Some female mice can raise a new family every 4 weeks.

mouse

The name "mouse" is used for many small RODENTS that are not necessarily closely related. Mice are found in almost every part of the world, and although most of them live in woods or grassy places, some mice come into houses to look for food, and they may even live indoors. Most mice are active at night. They eat seeds, nuts, and other plant foods.

mudskipper

Most fish cannot survive for long out of water, but finger-sized mudskippers are an exception to this rule. They live in tropical mangrove swamps in Africa and Asia, and at low tide they "skip" over the mud or climb up the exposed roots of the mangrove trees, searching for insects and small crustaceans. A mudskipper can survive in air because it has a large cavity around its gills which is filled with sea water. This sea water provides it with oxygen. See **lungfish**, **seashore**.

musk ox

These large grazing MAMMALS are adapted for life on the cold TUNDRA and have long shaggy coats that almost reach the ground. Musk oxen are found in northern Canada and Greenland. As a result of hunting, they are much less common than they once were. See **defense**.

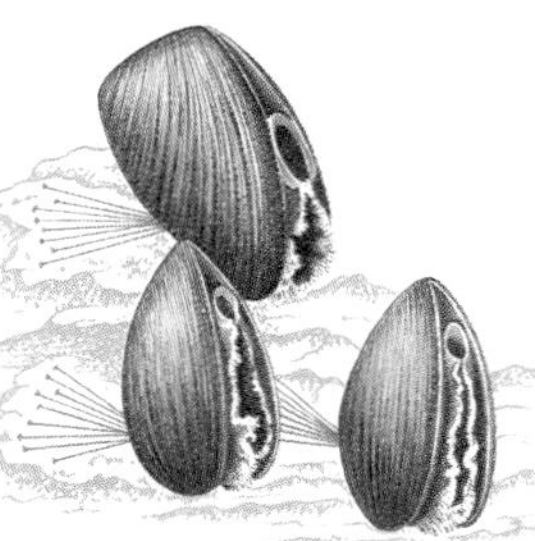

▶ A mussel eats by filtering small particles of food from water. It is attached to the rocks with tough threads.

mussel

Mussels are MOLLUSKS that live on rocky SEASHORES throughout the world. Like many other mollusks, mussels have a shell that protects their soft bodies. A mussel's shell has two parts that fit together, and the mussel keeps them shut if it is disturbed, or if the tide is out.

mynah

Mynahs are sociable noisy birds, related to STARLINGS. They are found in India, Sri Lanka, Southern Asia, New Guinea, and some of the Pacific islands, and they feed on fruit, insects, and lizards. The hill mynahs of India are often kept as cagebirds. They are wonderful mimics and can copy human speech perfectly.

▼ Mudskippers use their front fins like legs. The fin on a mudskipper's back works like a signal, and can be raised or lowered.

MOUNTAINS

Mountains are inhospitable places, because they are often cold and windy, with little shelter. Animals that live on mountains need to be hardy to cope with these difficult conditions. Mountain GOATS, SHEEP, and YAKS have thick shaggy coats to keep them warm, as well as special hooves that give them a firm grip on ice or smooth rock. They can digest tough plants, and this allows them to survive in the winter when there is no other food. Many predators that were once widespread, such as PUMAS, BEARS, and WOLVES, now survive only in the mountains. They have been killed or driven out of land lower down, and for them, mountains are a welcome refuge from a world dominated by humans.

MOUNTAIN FORESTS OF SOUTHEAST ASIA

The bamboo forests of China are the home of the giant panda. Today much of the bamboo has been cut down, and the giant panda would probably not survive without human help. The bamboo forests are also the home of the giant panda's "cousin," the red panda. This smaller animal eats a much wider range of food, so it has a better chance of surviving.

▼ The snow leopard has extra-long fur which protects it in winter, and during the cold nights at high altitude.

1 2 3 4 5 6

ANIMALS OF THE ANDES

Guanacos and vicuñas, two sure-footed mammals, are found only in the Andes. They are related to camels, and eat plants on high mountainsides. The Andean condor, one of the world's biggest birds, is also an Andean speciality, and so is the rare spectacled bear. The puma is found in North America as well, but is now very rare.

HIMALAYAN LIFE

1 Snow leopard
2 Apollo butterfly
3 Alpine chough
4 Nepalese swift
5 Golden eagle
6 Argali sheep
7 Yak
8 Lämmergeier
9 Himalayan ibex
10 Tibetan pika

MOUNTAIN WILDLIFE IN DANGER

At one time, it was very difficult to get to the Himalayas. Now, thanks to aircraft, thousands of climbers and trekkers visit these mountains every year. In the mountains, wood is often burned to cook food. With so many tourists visiting the mountains, the trees are disappearing fast. Trees are essential for mountain wildlife, because they provide food and hold on to the soil.

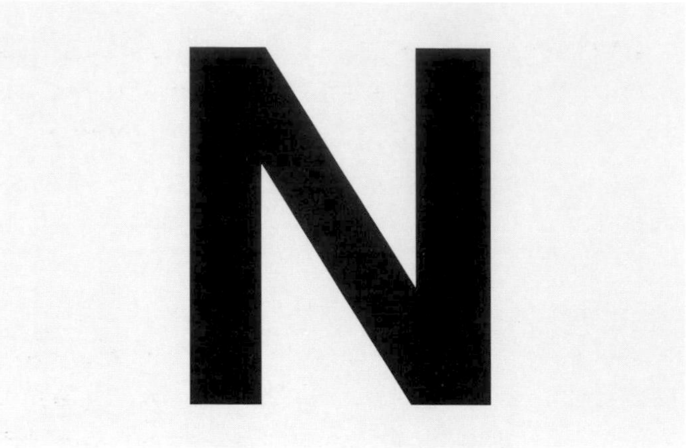

narwhal

Stories about unicorns probably owe their origin to the narwhal, a unique WHALE that has a long straight tusk sticking out from its upper jaw. This structure is actually a single tooth that grows very long and has spiral grooves. Narwhals live in the cold waters of the Arctic Ocean, and they eat fish, crustaceans, and squid.

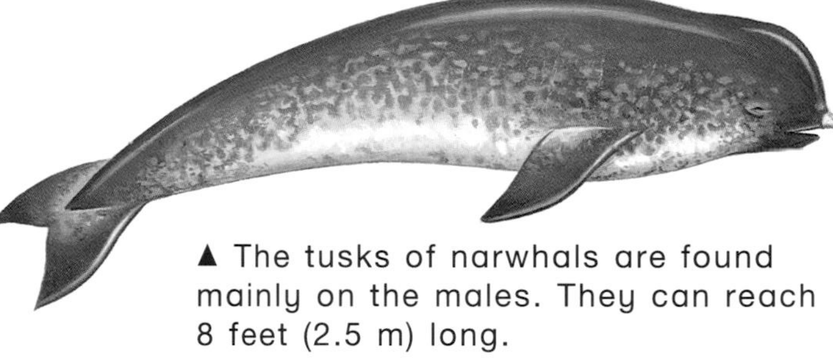

▲ The tusks of narwhals are found mainly on the males. They can reach 8 feet (2.5 m) long.

nature conservation see **conservation**

newt

Newts are small amphibians with spindly feet and long webbed tails. Unlike FROGS and TOADS, they spend a lot of their time in water. A newt uses its tail to swim, swishing it from side to side like a paddle. On land it walks rather slowly. Newts eat insects, earthworms, slugs, and small freshwater crustaceans. They are found in Europe and parts of Asia and North America. See **fresh water, salamander**.

nightjar

Hunting for moths and other flying insects in the fading evening light, a nightjar scoops up its prey in its gaping mouth. These unusual BIRDS have a ring of bristles around their mouths which helps them to trap insects. Nightjars are found in most parts of the world except Australia and New Zealand.

▲ A numbat has a long, sticky tongue and lots of small teeth.

numbat

This Australian MARSUPIAL feeds mainly on termites and ants. It grows to about 10 inches (26 cm) in length, excluding its long bristly tail. Numbats are unusual among marsupials because they have no pouch. Numbats are now very rare.

nuthatch

Insects hiding in the bark of trees are the main food of these small and agile BIRDS. Nuthatches have very large feet with sharp claws, and they run up and down branches and tree trunks as they search for their prey. Nuthatches are found in most parts of the world, except South America.

▶ A nuthatch can climb down trees as well as up.

oarfish

This unusual fish is long and ribbon-shaped, like a flattened EEL, and has two long red feelers below its head. The oarfish is found in deep sea waters.

ocelot

A medium-sized wild CAT with a beautiful spotted coat, the ocelot lives mainly in the forests of South and Central America. Ocelots are nocturnal and rarely seen.

▼ An octopus has a hard beak which is hidden away behind its tentacles. It kills crabs with a single bite.

octopus

These large-brained MOLLUSKS are the most intelligent of all INVERTEBRATES. Octopuses have eight tentacles, equipped with rows of suckers. Octopuses live in all the warmer oceans of the world, and some are found in cooler waters. See **squid**.

oilbird

Found only in Trinidad and the northernmost part of South America, oilbirds are nocturnal and spend the day in caves. At night they fly out into the forests to feed on fruit, especially that of the oil palm. In caves, oilbirds find their way by echolocation. See **bat**.

▲ The partly striped okapi hides away in the dense forests of central Africa.

okapi

The okapi lives in the rain forests of central Africa. This plant-eating MAMMAL is about the size of a small pony, and is a close relative of the GIRAFFE.

open seas see **pages 92 and 93**

opossum

The MARSUPIAL mammals of the Americas are known as opossums. They all have long pointed noses, and are quite small, although the Virginia opossum grows up to 20 inches (50 cm) long. See **possum**.

OPEN SEAS

In places, the oceans are several miles deep, and the animals that live at the surface are very different from those that live on or near the seabed. Near the surface there is plenty of light, and the water teems with small plants and animals. These provide food for fish and for corals. They are also scooped up by the largest of all sea animals, WHALES and the WHALE SHARK. The surface water can be a dangerous place, so some animals only come up to it after dark. In the ocean depths, food is very scarce and there is permanent darkness. Many deep-sea animals are scavengers, relying on leftovers that fall from the surface.

OCEAN BIRDS

Seabirds all have to breed on dry land, but some eat, drink, and even sleep far out in the oceans. Albatrosses can stay at sea for weeks, but frigate birds come back to land every evening to perch in trees. Instead of catching their own food, frigate birds steal it from other birds of the open sea.

▲ There are no plants in the deep sea, so fish have to live either on pieces of food that fall from the surface, or on each other. Many deep-sea fish produce their own light to lure prey. Some deep-sea eels can swallow fish that are twice their size.

▶ Three giants of the ocean world, the blue whale, the sperm whale, and the bowhead whale. The sperm whale has big teeth, and hunts giant squid. The two other whales do not have teeth. They feed by filtering small animals from the water.

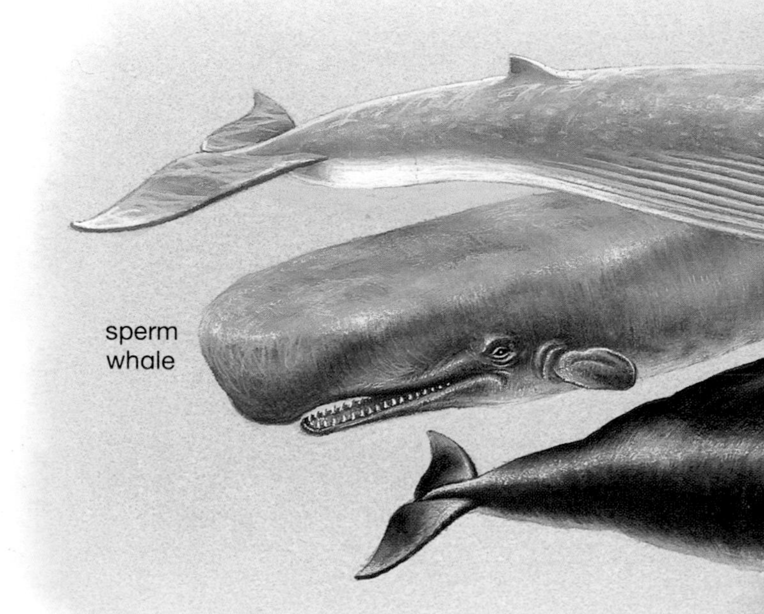

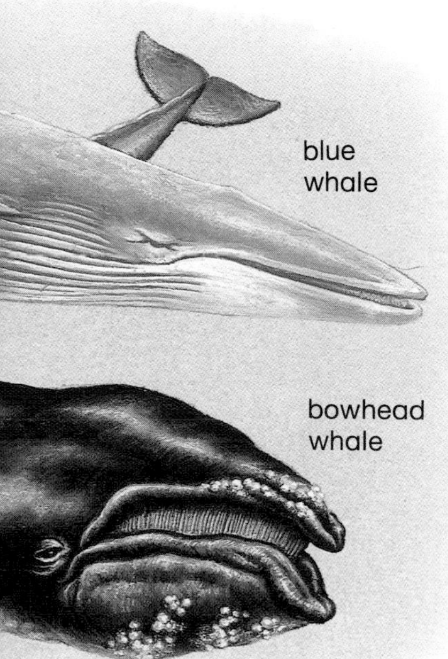

OCEANS IN DANGER

The oceans cover almost three-fourths of the Earth's surface. Despite their size, they cannot protect wildlife from humans. For years, people have dumped waste in the oceans. This causes pollution, which can kill fish and other animals. Fishing is also a serious threat. Some parts of the oceans are so heavily fished that there are very few large fish left.

▲ Corals look quite like plants, but they are actually small animals. A coral spends all its adult life in one place, and it often protects itself by building a hard case. Over thousands of years, their cases pile up to form huge banks, called coral reefs.

LIFE IN THE OPEN SEA

1 Starfish
2 Hammerhead shark
3 Blue shark
4 Barracuda
5 Sea urchin
6 Giant clam
7 Butterfly fish
8 Octopus
9 Seahorse
10 Manta ray
11 Squid

orangutan

This large and slow-moving ape lives in the rain forests of Southeast Asia. It spends nearly all its time in trees, and feeds on fruit, leaves, bark, termites, birds' eggs, and nestlings. Males are much bigger than females, and have a wide flap on either side of their faces.

▼ Orangutans are endangered by people who catch them and destroy their habitats.

oryx

Oryxes are a type of antelope, with very long slender horns that have a slight backward curve. Oryxes live mainly in Africa, and are well adapted to desert life.

osprey

Fish are the main food of the osprey, a medium-sized bird of prey. Ospreys are found all around the world wherever there are rivers, lakes, or sea coasts, except New Zealand.

ostrich

Ostriches are large flightless birds found on the dry plains of Africa. They can be over 8 feet (2.5 m) tall, and are the biggest birds in the world. Ostriches can run very quickly, reaching a speed of 40 miles (70 km) an hour. Ostriches eat seeds, fruit, leaves, insects, and small rodents.

▲ Otters have webbed feet, and they can close their ears and nostrils when they swim.

otter

All otters live close to water. These agile and fast-swimming mammals feed on fish, frogs, crayfish, and crabs, and even on young waterbirds. There are twelve kinds of otter around the world, and the sea otter of North America is the only one that spends nearly all of its time at sea. Most otters are becoming rarer because of water pollution and disturbances.

▼ Owls have special wing feathers which make their flight silent. In the dark this makes their attack a complete surprise.

owl

Owls are hunting birds that are found throughout the world. Unlike birds of prey, they hunt mainly after dark. Owls have superb hearing and eyesight which allows them to swoop down on their prey in dim light, or even darkness.

oxpecker

These lively birds, with their bright red or yellow beaks, are found only in Africa. They live among grazing animals, such as buffalo, rhinoceroses, antelope, and zebra, and often scuttle about over their bodies looking for food. Oxpeckers eat small parasites, known as ticks.

panda

The giant panda of China is one of the best known animals in the world. It is an unusual type of BEAR that has abandoned the usual diet of bears—a mixture of fruit, meat, and fish—to feed solely on bamboo shoots. At one time, large areas of bamboo covered the mountains of China, and pandas thrived. Since then, much of the bamboo has been removed, and there are now few places left with enough bamboo to keep a giant panda alive. See **conservation, red panda**.

◀ Many giant pandas are kept in zoos. It is very difficult to tell male and female pandas apart, so encouraging them to breed is often difficult. So far, only a few baby pandas have been born in captivity.

pangolin

Pangolins are covered with overlapping bony scales that make them look like huge walking pine cones. Found in Africa and parts of Asia, they eat ants and termites. Some pangolins are ground-dwellers, while others climb up into trees. A pangolin's scales have sharp edges, and protect it from enemies. See **mammal**.

parasite

A parasite is a small animal that lives on or inside another animal and feeds on its "host." Some parasites, such as tapeworms, stay with one animal for all their adult lives. Others, such as FLEAS and MOSQUITOES, move from one host to another. They stay for as long as several weeks, or as little as a few seconds. Almost all animals have parasites. Some parasites cause little harm, but others can be deadly. See **animal partnerships**.

parental care see **page 96**

▶ Many parrots, including lovebirds and parakeets, are kept as cage birds. They are brought from their homes in the tropics. This is an African gray parrot.

parrot

Most parrots are colorful tree-dwelling BIRDS that eat fruit, seeds, or flowers. They have strong claws and short, hooked beaks which they can use like hands when climbing about in the trees. The largest parrots are the MACAWS of South America, while the smallest are the pygmy parrots of New Guinea. Parrots mainly live in warmer climates.

PARENTAL CARE

When a HERRING releases its eggs, it swims away and has no more to do with them. But many parent animals do not behave like this. Instead, they have far fewer offspring, and they spend at least some of their time helping their young to survive. Parental care is shown by many kinds of animal. All MAMMALS care for their young by feeding them, and so do many BIRDS. Lots of animals, from GREBES to SCORPIONS, carry their young about, so that they are not exposed to their enemies. Young animals often learn important skills while they are with their parents, so once they start living on their own they are better able to survive. See **behavior**.

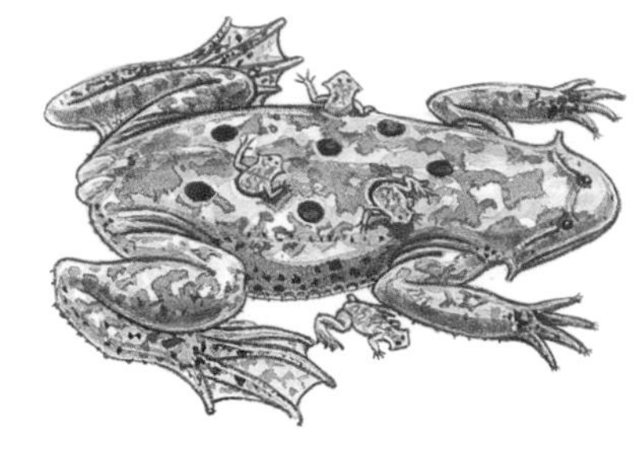

◀ When a female Surinam toad lays eggs, the male presses them onto her back. She carries the eggs until they hatch.

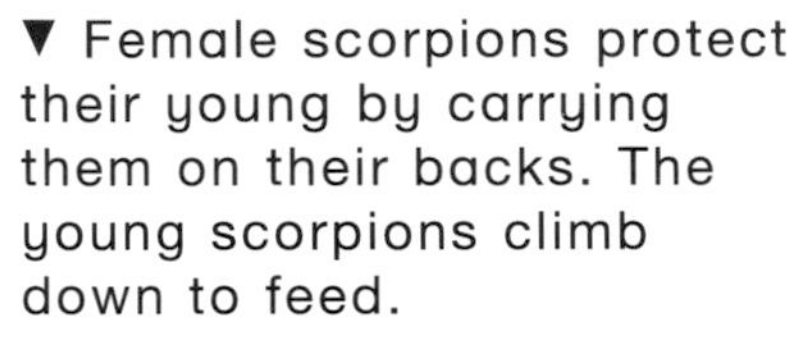

▼ Female scorpions protect their young by carrying them on their backs. The young scorpions climb down to feed.

◀ Young mice rely on their mother for food. She feeds them with milk until they are old enough to find food themselves.

◀ A young kangaroo, or joey, spends the first months of its life in the protection of its mother's pouch. The mother kangaroo often has a young joey in her pouch, and an older joey close by.

▶ Some water-birds, like mergansers and grebes, look after their young by carrying them on their backs. This keeps the young birds warm, and also protects them from enemies such as pike, which lurk close to the surface.

partridge
These stocky ground-dwelling BIRDS feed on seeds and insects. Partridges only take to the air as a last resort, and usually run for cover if disturbed. They live in farmland, grassland, scrub, and moorland in many parts of the world.

peacock
The peacock is well known for his large and beautiful "tail," which he displays when courting the female. The tail is actually short, but special feathers in front of it fan out when it is raised. The female, or peahen, is much duller in color. Peacocks come from India and Sri Lanka.

▲ A peacock uses his tail to attract a female. He opens out the feathers, and then shakes them to make a rustling sound.

peafowl see **peacock**

peccary
Peccaries are small piglike animals that live mainly in tropical and subtropical regions of the Americas. They dig for roots and bulbs, and also take any small animals they come across. Peccaries do not have good eyesight, but they have a very good sense of smell.

▶ White pelicans beat the water with their wings to drive the fish toward the shore.

pelican
A pelican is a large BIRD with a pouch beneath its beak. The pouch is made of stretchy skin. A feeding pelican scoops up a beakful of water and fish, then squeezes the water out of the pouch through the sides of its beak. It then swallows the fish that are trapped inside.

penguin
Although they cannot fly, penguins are superb swimmers. These BIRDS use their short stubby wings as flippers, and their stubby feet work like rudders to steer through the water. Penguins are found only in the Southern Hemisphere.

perch
Perch are FISH found in a variety of FRESH WATER habitats, from small streams and rivers to large lakes and canals. They prey on smaller fish and invertebrates. They lay their eggs in strings around the stems of plants.

▶ A perch has spiny rays in its back fin.

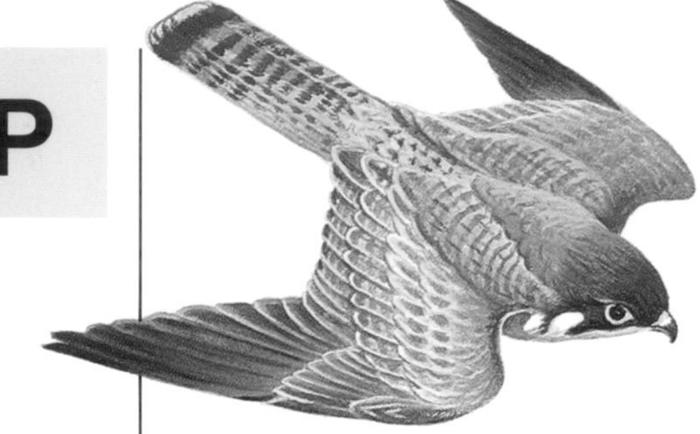

◀ During a dive, a peregrine can reach a speed of about 110 mph (180 km/h). This is faster than any other bird.

peregrine
This small FALCON is a very successful BIRD OF PREY and is found in most parts of the world. It prefers areas with mountains or cliffs, where it can build its nest on a rock ledge. Peregrines hunt by swooping onto other birds at high speed, and striking them with their claws.

phalanger see **possum**

pheasant
Pheasants are large ground-dwelling BIRDS that feed on seeds, insects, and other small animals. Pheasants originally lived in the forests of Asia, but they have been introduced to many other places.

▼ The male common pheasant has a brightly colored head and long tail. The female is more drab.

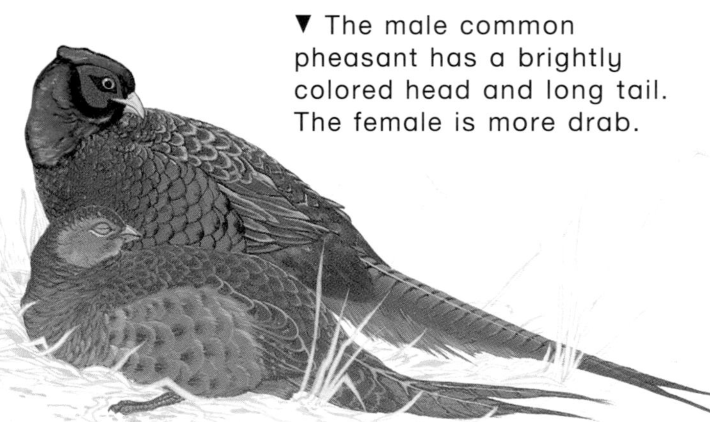

pig
Unlike farmyard pigs, most wild pigs are hairy with rough bristly coats. They live mainly in forests, and eat a great variety of food, including roots, fallen fruit, nuts, shoots, leaves, grain, insects, and young birds. Some pigs eat the remains of dead animals as well. They have muscular snouts for rooting in the earth, and their young often have stripy coats.

pigeon
The gentle coo-cooing sound made by pigeons and doves can be heard in almost every country of the world. These fruit- and seed-eating BIRDS are found in forests, in farmland, gardens, and rocky places, and they are also very common in some cities. City pigeons are descended from domesticated birds.

▲ The pike's dappled colors hide it among water plants. It rushes forward to attack with a flick of its powerful tail.

pike
A large fierce predatory FISH, the pike lives in rivers and lakes throughout Europe, Asia, and North America. It has a long, flattened snout and large jaws. As well as feeding on fish, it also eats small mammals, such as water voles, ducklings, and the young of other water-birds.
The pike has a powerful tail, and catches its prey with a sudden lunge.

pilot fish
These small FISH are found in the oceans, wherever there are large SHARKS and RAYS. They swim close to a shark or ray, and often ahead of it, waiting to share the morsels of food that are scattered when the larger fish makes a kill.

▲ Most piranhas are only about 1 foot (30 cm) long, but have needle-sharp teeth.

piranha

In the Amazon river, piranhas are greatly feared. A large school of these FISH can eat a human being in a few minutes, each fish taking small bites with its sharp teeth. However, attacks like this happen very rarely. Piranhas mainly eat other fish or dead animals that have fallen into the water.

plaice

The plaice is a large European flounder that spends all of its adult life lying on the seabed. It is palc underneath, but its upper side is beautifully camouflaged to match the sand and mud around it. Plaice live in the Atlantic Ocean.

▼ Polar bears catch seals through holes in the ice.

platypus

The duck-billed platypus is one of the strangest MAMMALS on Earth, found only in Australia. It is a monotreme—one of the very few mammals that lay eggs. It is specialized for an underwater life, and has a large horny plate extending from each jaw, exactly like a duck's bill. The platypus uses this for churning up the muddy bottoms of rivers and lakes so that it can catch crustaceans and insects.

▲ The platypus's bill is soft and sensitive. The bill scoops up small animals that live in underwater mud.

pocket gopher

These rat-sized RODENTS eat the parts of plants that they find while burrowing underground. There are 30 species, found only in North America, and most are rather ugly animals with very large teeth and snouts. Gophers harm vegetation, and can be a problem on farmland.

polar bear

The white-coated polar bear lives in the Arctic, and roams the tundra and pack-ice, or swims powerfully through the icy water. Polar bears live almost entirely on other animals, although in the summer they manage to add some leaves and berries to their diet. They catch seals, fish, Arctic hares, foxes, and reindeer. Polar bears give birth to up to four cubs in dens, which are often hollowed out in the snow.

POLAR REGIONS

The Earth's two polar regions—the Arctic and Antarctic—are quite different, and they have their own separate wildlife. The Antarctic is a huge island that is almost completely covered by ice, while the Arctic is a frozen sea, almost surrounded by land. In both polar regions, the sea is full of wildlife. The Antarctic is the home of PENGUINS, which dive for food from the floating ice. The Arctic is the home of the WALRUS and the NARWHAL, and also of the POLAR BEAR, which migrates southward to the TUNDRA during winter. In the Antarctic there is no adjoining tundra, and so large land animals like the polar bear cannot survive there.

PLANKTON

The icy water around the poles is full of small plants and animals. This mass of floating life is called plankton. It includes shrimplike krill, which are the food of penguins and whales.

LIFE IN THE ANTARCTIC

1 Emperor penguin
2 Crab-eater seal
3 Adélie penguin
4 Skua
5 Sheathbill

WHALES AND DOLPHINS

These mammals have adapted to life in water. They still breathe air, but instead of legs, they have flippers. All dolphins, and small whales like the narwhal, have teeth. They are hunters and feed mainly on fish. Large whales like the bowhead filter plankton. A curtain of fringed fibers, called baleen plates, filters plankton from the water.

THE ANTARCTIC IN DANGER

The Antarctic is the coldest place on Earth. Until recently, very few people had ever visited it. The Antarctic contains minerals, which some people want to mine. So far, mining has not been allowed. If it does happen, it could endanger the continent and wildlife.

LIFE IN THE ARCTIC

1 King eider
2 Ringed seal
3 Polar bear
4 Little auk
5 Razorbill

◀ A polecat's body is slender, allowing it to hunt other animals in their burrows.

polecat

Closely related to the WEASELS and STOATS, polecats are long-bodied animals with short legs and sharply pointed faces. They also have the same lively curiosity and nimble movements. Polecats live in a variety of regions, from forests to steppes and semi-deserts. They hunt for small animals including insects, mice, voles, birds, and lizards. The domestic FERRET is descended from the polecat of Europe.

pondskater (water strider)

These slender black INSECTS are light enough to rest on the surface of water without sinking into it. They move about with rapid beats of their hind legs, propelling themselves across the surface in a jerky rhythm. Pondskaters feed on small insects.

▶ Porcupines live in North and South America, Africa, India, and in parts of Asia and Europe.

porcupine

All porcupines have sharp spines that they use to defend themselves. Some porcupines have very short spines only a little longer than their fur. Others, such as the crested porcupine of Africa, have very long spines. Porcupines are RODENTS, and they mainly eat plants.

porcupine fish

Like PORCUPINES on land, this small FISH is covered with sharp spines. However, it also has another trick for deterring enemies: it can inflate its body into a large spiky ball.

▲ A porcupine fish feeds on shellfish.

porpoise

Porpoises are small sea MAMMALS and are related to the WHALES and DOLPHINS. They rarely grow more than 6 feet (2 m) in length, and unlike dolphins, they do not have beaklike jaws. There are six species of porpoise, all of which live in the northern hemisphere, usually in coastal waters. Squid and fish are their main food.

Portuguese man-of-war

Although it looks rather like a JELLYFISH, the Portuguese man-of-war is a collection of small animals, and belongs to a group called the siphonophores. It has a large air-filled float, with long stinging tentacles hanging down below. Fish and other animals that swim among the tentacles are stung and paralyzed, then slowly hauled in and digested.

possum

Possums are cat-sized climbing MARSUPIALS that can wrap their tails around branches. The brush-tailed possum of Australia lives in woodland, and feeds on leaves and fruit. Other possums, called phalangers, live in the islands north of Australia.

prairie dog

The prairie dog is not a dog at all, but a plump RODENT that lives in burrows in the GRASSY PLAINS of North America. Prairie dogs are very sociable animals, and they build large "cities" of connected tunnels. Each city has many entrance holes, and a special ventilating system that ensures a supply of fresh air underground. Prairie dogs feed on grass, and they gather stores of food to see them through the winter.

▼ At the first sign of an enemy such as a bird of prey, a guard gives a loud bark, and all the prairie dogs scamper underground.

prawn

Prawns are found in seas and oceans all over the world. Most of these small shrimplike CRUSTACEANS are scavengers, taking scraps of plant and animal food.

▶ Prawns have long antennae, and slender claws. Some prawns are completely transparent.

praying mantis

These predatory INSECTS have powerful barbed forearms which they hold together, like someone holding their hands in prayer. If an insect comes within reach, the mantis suddenly strikes, and its forearms snap shut to hold its victim.

▶ A barbary macaque is a typical primate. Its eyes both point forward, and it has flat nails instead of claws. Macaques live mainly on the ground.

primates

Primates are MAMMALS that have flexible fingers and toes. We are primates, and so are APES, MONKEYS, and LEMURS, together with several smaller animals such as LORISES and TARSIERS. Primates probably evolved from small insect-eating animals called TREE SHREWS, about 60 million years ago. The first primates were nocturnal. However, primates gradually became active in the daytime, and they evolved good vision which enabled them to judge distances when jumping from branches.

P

processionary moth

The caterpillars of processionary moths live together in a large communal nest made of silk threads, which is suspended in a tree. They get their name because they walk to their feeding area each morning in a long procession, one behind the other. They lay strands of silk as they go and follow the track back when they have finished.

◀ Processionary moth caterpillars eat leaves. They can cause great damage in forests in parts of the world with warm summers.

pronghorn

This unusual animal is a member of a group of grazing animals called the antilocaprids. These animals were very successful between 2 and 5 million years ago but all are now extinct, except the pronghorn. The pronghorn lives on the prairies of North America, and in some desert areas.

▲ Pronghorns rely on speed to escape danger.

protozoans

Protozoans are all single-celled creatures that cannot be seen without a microscope. Protozoans have more in common with animals than plants, because they have to find their own food. However they are usually classified as a completely separate group. Some protozoans are PARASITES that cause diseases.

puffin

Puffins have bright red feet, and during the breeding season, they also have brightly colored beaks. They nest in burrows in the grassy turf near the edge of sea cliffs. Puffins dig burrows for themselves, using their feet, or take over those made by RABBITS, and they lay a single egg. Puffins are found in the cooler parts of the northern hemisphere.

▶ Puffins dive for small fish. A puffin's beak can hold up to a dozen fish, with their heads and tails facing alternate directions.

PROTOZOANS

Protozoans usually live in water or damp places, and they move in different ways. Some beat tiny hairs, called flagella or cilia, which work like paddles. Others move by changing shape.

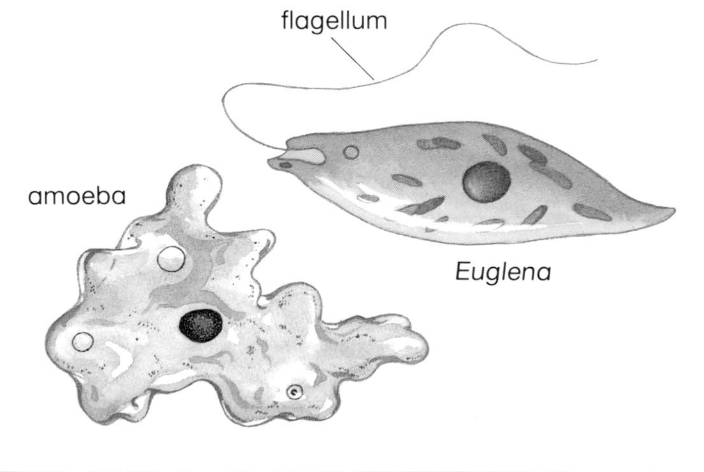

◀ In North America, hunting has brought the puma close to extinction.

puma

Also known as the mountain lion or cougar, this member of the CAT family grows to 5 feet (1.6 m) in length. Pumas prey on a variety of animals, from small mice to large deer. Although adult pumas have plain tawny coats, their cubs are spotted.

▶ The largest pythons grow up to 33 feet (10 m) long. Pythons live in forests, scrub and mangrove swamps.

python

Pythons are related to the BOAS of the Americas. At up to 33 feet (10 m), the beautifully patterned reticulated python of Southeast Asia may be the world's longest snake. Some pythons kill by wrapping their bodies around their victims; other pythons kill by biting with their teeth. Pythons are found in the tropics of Africa, Asia, and Australia. See **boa constrictor**.

quelea

There are probably more queleas in the world than any other kind of BIRD. Queleas are related to SPARROWS, and have brown bodies and red bills. They live in the grasslands and woodland of Africa, feeding on wild seeds or farmers' grain. Queleas can form flocks containing up to 10,000 birds which can ruin food crops, and cause so much damage that they are compared to swarms of locusts. Queleas nest very close together, sometimes with several hundred nests in one tree.

▼ Queleas breed very quickly, and are very hard to control. They probably make up a tenth of all the birds on Earth.

rabbit

In terms of numbers, rabbits are among the most successful MAMMALS in the world. They feed on plants and, like RODENTS, they have sharp front teeth that never stop growing. They use their teeth to cut through grass and leaves. See **hare**.

▲ Wild raccoons live near wooded streams or swamps, but many have taken up life in towns.

raccoon

Raccoons are very adaptable MAMMALS that live in North America. They usually search for food at night and rest during the daytime. Raccoons have learned that garbage cans contain food, and they do well on the outskirts of towns.

raft spider

Not many spiders live in water, but raft spiders do and they even catch small fish. A raft spider lurks among the leaves of floating plants, and waits for animals to come past. See **water spider**.

rain forests see **pages 108 and 109**

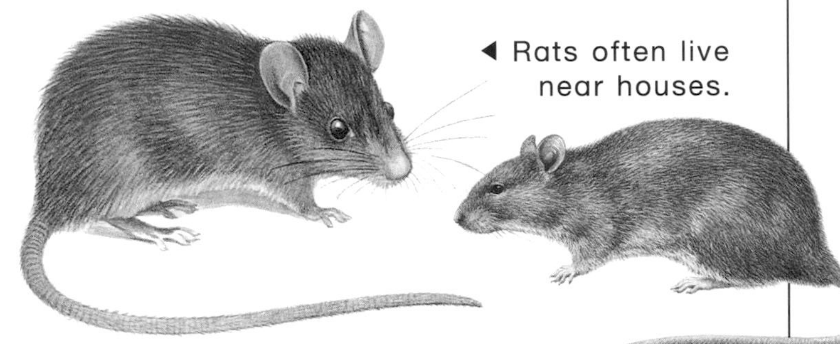

◀ Rats often live near houses.

rat

The name "rat" is used for many different RODENTS that have large bodies and bare tails. The black rat carries fleas that can pass on bubonic plague, a disease that has killed millions of people around the world. The brown rat can transmit other serious diseases.

▶ A rattlesnake has several hollow bony rings at the end of its tail. When the snake shakes its tail from side to side, the rings make a rattling or buzzing sound.

rattlesnake

Rattlesnakes are fat-bodied SNAKES with short wide heads. They are found in North and South America, mainly in DESERTS, and they produce a powerful venom that they use to kill small mammals and birds. They have special tails that can make a warning sound.

raven

The largest members of the CROW family, ravens are glossy black birds seen mostly in mountain areas. They eat many kinds of food, and are found in the cooler parts of the northern hemisphere, as far north as the Arctic.

ray

Rays are strange kite-shaped FISH that often have long whiplike tails. They are related to SHARKS and have a skeleton made of rubbery cartilage instead of bone. Rays live in most of the world's oceans. They feed on shellfish on the seabed.

▶ A ray has very wide fins on the sides of its body. It beats its fins like wings.

red deer

This large species of DEER is found throughout the cooler regions of the northern hemisphere, from Canada to western China. In North America it is known as the elk or wapiti. Red deer are very adaptable animals and can live in woodland or on open moorland and mountainsides.

▶ The red panda feeds on bamboo shoots and fruit, acorns, grass, mice, and birds.

red panda

Despite its name, the red or lesser panda is not very closely related to the giant PANDA. Instead, it looks rather like a rust-colored RACCOON and has the same banded tail. The red panda lives in China and some other parts of Asia.

reindeer

Called caribou in North America, these large DEER are found all around the Arctic. Reindeer live in herds, and eat leaves and lichens. They are the only deer species in which the female also has antlers.

remora

Remoras are small FISH that attach themselves to SHARKS by special suckers on their heads. In this way, they are able to travel great distances through the oceans without making any effort. Remoras eat some of the PARASITES living on the shark, but they also catch prey, such as smaller fish and crustaceans.

▼ During the breeding season, male deer use their antlers to battle with each other.

RAIN FORESTS

Tropical rain forests have a greater variety of animal life than any other HABITAT. This is because there is plenty of sunlight and rain, so that plants can grow all year round. The trees and creepers provide a non-stop supply of leaves and fruit. Among the fruit-eaters are SPIDER MONKEYS, FLYING FOXES, PARROTS, and the strange OILBIRD. Other MONKEYS and APES eat leaves, and there are huge numbers of caterpillars that eventually turn into BUTTERFLIES AND MOTHS. Tree SNAKES prey on small animals, and on the dark forest floor, PECCARIES, TAPIRS, and CAPYBARAS search for fallen fruit and nuts, while JAGUARS and LEOPARDS stalk them through the shade.

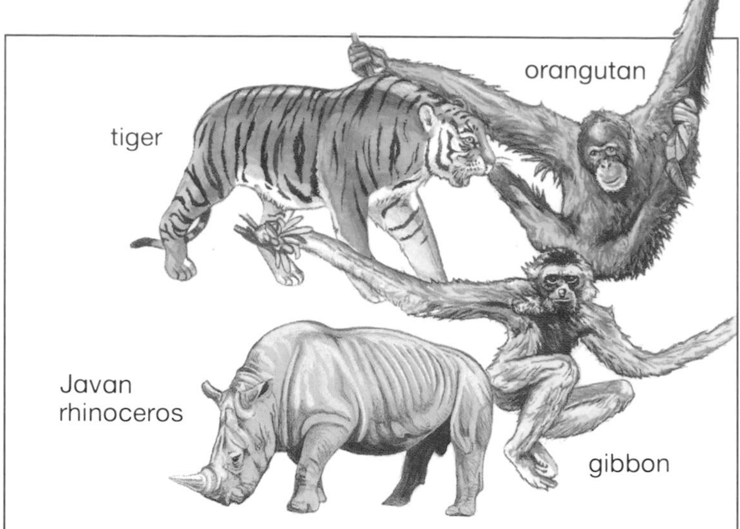

RAIN FORESTS OF SOUTHEAST ASIA

At dawn, the rain forests in Southeast Asia echo with the hooting of gibbons, high in the treetops. These forests are also the home of a much rarer ape, the orangutan, which moves slowly through the trees. Tigers were once common in these forests, but are now rarely seen. The Sumatran rhinoceros feeds on leaves and wallows in wet mud during the heat of the day.

RAIN FORESTS IN DANGER

The trees in a rain forest provide food for animals. They also hold the soil in place. In many places, rain forests are being cut down for timber, and to make room for farms. Once the trees have gone, all the forest's wildlife disappears too.

R

REPRODUCTION

All animals have to reproduce. Some simple animals, such as PROTOZOANS, pull themselves in half. Each of the halves then becomes a new animal. More complicated animals usually need two parents to reproduce. The female makes the eggs, and the male fertilizes the eggs with cells called sperm. In many FISH and other water animals, the eggs and sperm are shed into the water. But in REPTILES, BIRDS, and MAMMALS, the male fertilizes the eggs while they are still in the mother's body. See **parental care**.

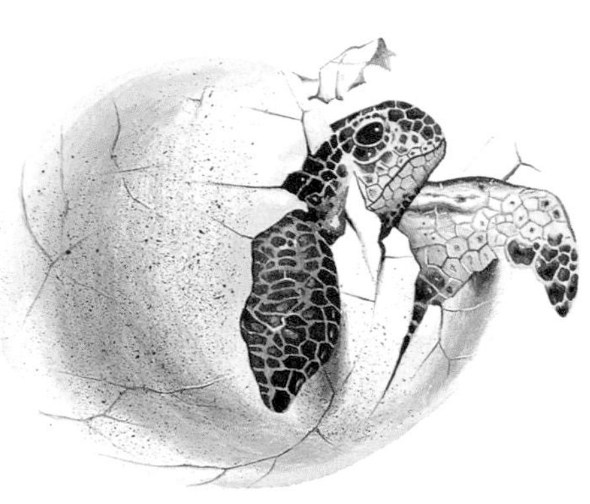

▶ Turtles mate in the sea, but the female lays her eggs in a hole which she digs in a sandy beach. The baby turtles hatch and scuttle into the sea.

▼ A male frog fertilizes the eggs as the female lays them (1). The eggs produce tadpoles (2), which slowly turn into adults (3).

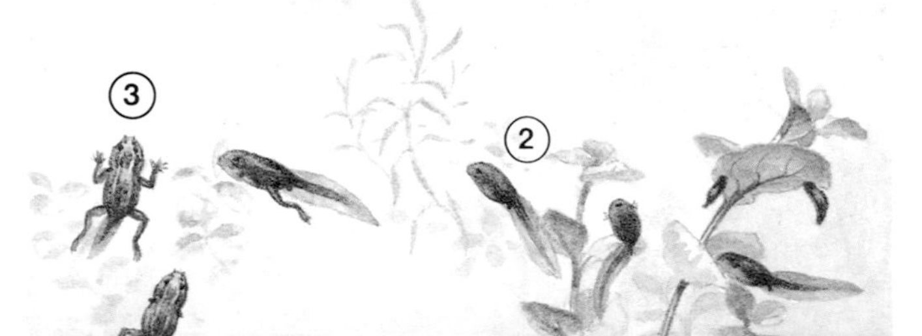

▶ A male stickleback makes an underwater nest, and the female fish lays her eggs inside. After the eggs have hatched, the father looks after them.

▼ A female bison usually gives birth to just one calf.

R

reptiles

A hundred million years ago, the largest and strongest animals on Earth were reptiles—mainly dinosaurs. The dinosaurs all became extinct, and today only TORTOISES, TURTLES, CROCODILES, ALLIGATORS, LIZARDS, and SNAKES still survive. All reptiles have scaly skin and are cold-blooded. They have to bask in the sunshine if the air is cold, because they cannot stay warm as we can. Most reptiles reproduce by laying eggs with leathery shells, but with some reptiles the eggs hatch in the mother's body.

REPTILES

Most reptiles are hunters, although turtles and tortoises often eat plant food. Reptiles need warmth to become active, and cannot live in places that are cold.

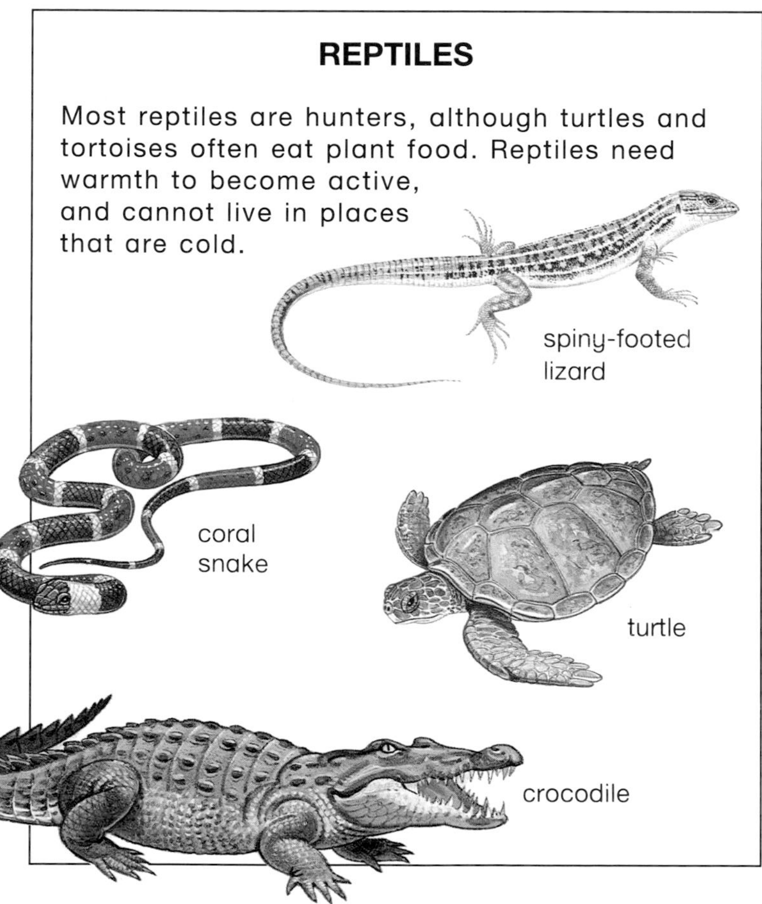

rhea

The rhea is a flightless South American BIRD. It lives in grassland where it feeds on seeds, leaves and small animals. Rheas stand about 5 feet (1.5 m) tall.

▲ The black rhinoceros is one of the world's most endangered large mammals. Without protection, it may soon become extinct.

rhinoceros

Rhinoceroses are heavy MAMMALS that have horns, thick skin, and usually little body hair. There are 5 kinds of rhinoceros, and the biggest of them—the white and black rhinoceros—both live in Africa, and have two horns. The Indian rhinoceros, which is the largest species in Asia, has just one. Unfortunately for rhinoceroses, some people think that their horns have magical properties. Many rhinos have been killed for their horns, bringing them close to extinction.

right whale

Right whales can reach 60 feet (18 m) in length, but are fairly slow swimmers, making them easy to catch. There are three species found in the cold waters bordering the Arctic and Antarctic. They are baleen whales, feeding on tiny shrimplike animals which they catch near the sea's surface on the long fringed plates in their huge mouths.

▲ Roadrunners are related to cuckoos and live in semi-deserts in the southern United States.

roadrunner

Although the roadrunner cannot match the speed of the OSTRICH, it can sprint along at up to 17 miles (28 km) an hour, an impressive speed for a BIRD whose body is only 21 inches (55 cm) long. It uses its speed to escape from danger, and also to catch lizards and snakes.

robin

The Old World robin is a small insect-eating BIRD with an orangey-red breast. It lives in European woods and gardens, and in North Africa and Asia, and belongs to the THRUSH family. The North American robin also belongs to the thrush family, but is a larger, different bird.

rodents

This large and very successful group of MAMMALS includes many different animals with chisel-like front teeth that never stop growing. Most rodents are fairly small, although the BEAVER grows to 5 feet (1.5 m), while some of the South American rodents, such as the CAPYBARA, are very large indeed. Most rodents live at ground level, hiding in burrows during the day and feeding in the open at night. Rodents generally feed on seeds and plants, and they can breed very quickly.

rook

The sooty black rook is a noisy member of the CROW family that lives near farmland in Europe and the northern parts of Asia. Rooks live in groups, and build their nests in "rookeries" at the tops of tall trees. They eat many kinds of food. See **birds**.

▶ Rooks eat many kinds of food, including eggs, grain, and other crops. Although they are thought of as pests, they also help farmers by eating insects and their grubs.

ruminants

Most MAMMALS cannot digest the useful part of leaves. Ruminants get around this problem by using bacteria and PROTOZOANS to do the digesting for them. Ruminants include animals such as BUFFALO, ANTELOPE, SHEEP, and DEER. They have a special stomach chamber, called a rumen, which is full of millions of tiny organisms. These organisms break down the leaves so that a ruminant gets the most out of its food.

▼ Rodents use their sharp teeth to chew through food, and anything in their way. A beaver can chew through trees, and a mouse can chew through electrical cables.

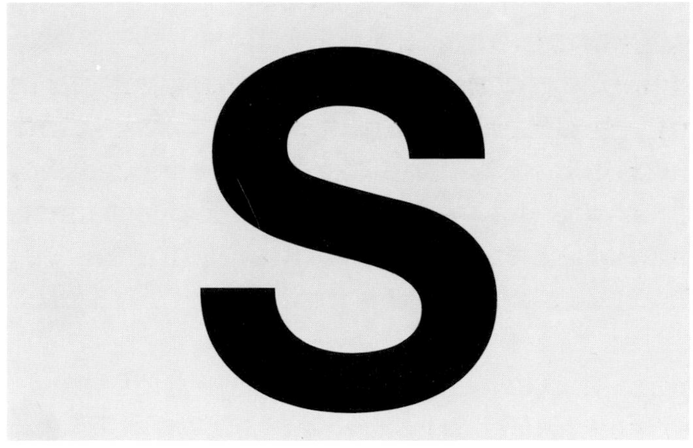

saiga
The saiga is an unusual looking MAMMAL, related to the GOAT. It has short horns and a long swollen nose. The saiga's nose may help to warm up air that it breathes in, allowing it to survive in its home on the cold GRASSY PLAINS of central Asia.

sailfish
This powerful FISH gets its name from the very tall fin, rather like the sail of a boat, that runs all the way along its back. It uses this fin to herd together schools of small fish, which it then eats.

▲ Many salamanders have bright colors that warn that their skin is poisonous.

salamander
Salamanders are AMPHIBIANS. They have rubbery bodies and long tails, and feed on worms, insects, snails, and slugs. Most salamanders spend some time on land but return to ponds, lakes, or rivers to lay their eggs.

▲ Salmon are found throughout the northern hemisphere. They have powerful bodies and can leap over quite large waterfalls.

salmon
Most FISH live either in the sea or in FRESH WATER, but salmon migrate from one to the other. A salmon begins life in a stream and slowly moves down toward the sea, often taking several years to get there. In the sea, it feeds on smaller fish such as herring. To breed, it makes its way back to the place where it hatched, finding its home river by the "scent" of its water. Many salmon die after breeding.

sand dollar
Sand dollars are flat SEA URCHINS that look like large coins. They live in muddy seabeds in shallow water and collect particles of food from the water.
See **echinoderms**.

▼ A sand dollar lives half-buried in sand.

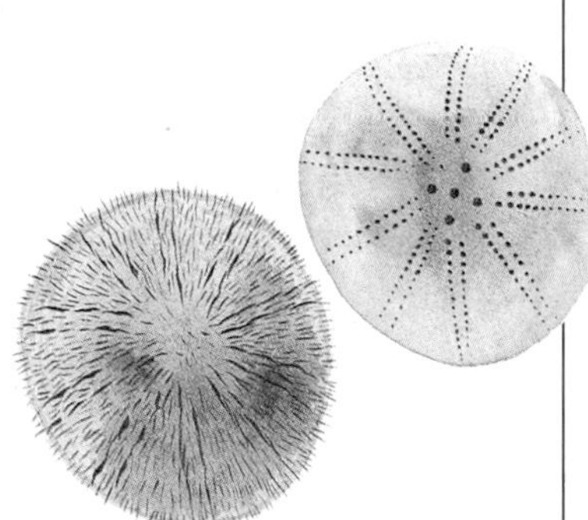

sapsucker
As their name suggests, these BIRDS live partly on a diet of sap, which they get by pecking holes in trees. A sapsucker drills holes in a tree, and then returns at regular intervals to drink the sap and take any insects that have been attracted by it. Sapsuckers are closely related to WOODPECKERS, and are found in woods, gardens, and orchards from Canada south to the Caribbean.

sawfish

The long flattened snout of the sawfish has a row of sharp teeth along each side. By lashing its body, the sawfish can inflict serious wounds on its enemies, and can also stun and injure the small fish on which it feeds. Sawfish are found throughout the world's oceans, except in very cold waters.

◀ Sawfish are close relatives of rays. Like rays, they have wide front fins, and flattened bodies.

sawfly

Sawflies are small INSECTS that are related to WASPS and ANTS. Some look like very slender wasps, although they do not have a narrow waist. Adult sawflies feed on nectar. Sawflies get their name because the female lays eggs through a special tube that has sawlike teeth.

scorpion

The powerful sting in a scorpion's tail has made these INVERTEBRATES greatly feared. Scorpions are related to the spiders. They have flattened bodies and two powerful pincers. They live mainly in the tropics, and they feed on insects, spiders, and centipedes. See **arachnids**, **parental care**.

▶ Scorpions use their stings to paralyze large insects, and to defend themselves.

sea anemone

Sea anemones are animals that belong to the group called the COELENTERATES. They live on coasts, and usually fasten themselves to rocks with a special sucker. Sea anemones have a ring of stinging tentacles which they trail in the water. If a small animal touches a tentacle, it is paralyzed by tiny stinging threads, and pulled toward the anemone's mouth. See **animal partnerships**.

▶ A sea anemone's mouth is surrounded by tentacles. Each one is armed with thousands of stinging threads.

seacow

Also known as a dugong, this barrel-shaped sea MAMMAL lives in coastal waters around Africa, India, Southeast Asia, New Guinea, northern Australia, and some of the Pacific islands. It feeds on water plants, and its closest living relatives are the ELEPHANTS.

seagull

Seagulls are adaptable BIRDS that live along coasts and often far inland. They have long narrow wings, are expert gliders, and often travel long distances with very little effort. At one time, seagulls lived on what they found near the shore. Today, many seagulls find food around garbage dumps and fishing boats.

seahorse
Seahorses are small and unusual FISH that are covered with bony armor. They move extremely slowly by flapping their tiny fins. When they need to stay still, they often curl their thin tails around water plants for anchorage.

▼ A female seahorse lays her eggs into a pouch on the front of the male's body. He takes care of them until they hatch.

seal
Seals are MAMMALS with streamlined bodies and powerful flippers. They can hold their breath for several minutes during a dive. Although they feed at sea, all seals have to return to land to breed. On land, they move quite slowly. Seals are found in all the oceans of the world.

▶ Seals breed on remote shores, and they usually return to the same breeding beaches every year.

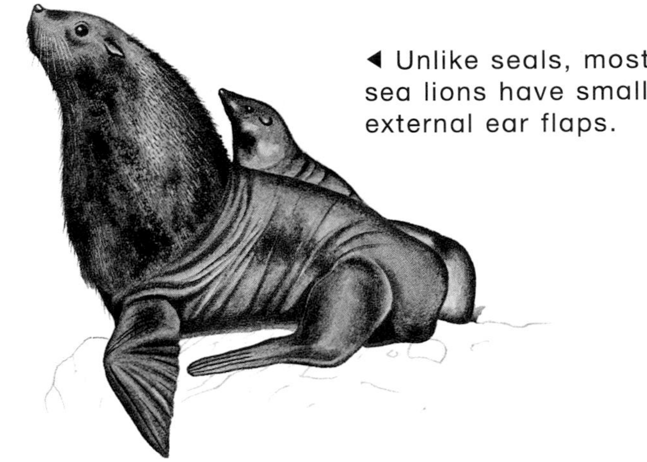
◀ Unlike seals, most sea lions have small external ear flaps.

sea lion
Sea lions look much like their relatives the SEALS, but their hindlimbs can move forward to act like stubby legs, enabling them to lift their bodies off the ground. Sea lions feed on fish, squid, and other sea animals. Some sea lions have thick fur.

seashore see **pages 116 and 117**

sea snake
Sea snakes have flattened bodies and a tail that works like an oar. Most sea snakes eat fish or fish eggs and have a poisonous bite. They are found only in tropical seas. See **snake**.

sea urchin
Sea urchins belong to the animal group called the ECHINODERMS, and have a thin outer casing covered with brittle spines. Some feed on tiny plants that grow on the surface of rocks, while others eat small animals. See **sand dollar**.

secretary bird
This long-legged BIRD looks rather like an EAGLE on stilts. It stands 5 feet (1.5 m) tall and stalks its prey in the plains of Africa. A secretary bird kills rodents, snakes, and lizards by stamping on them.

SEASHORE

Not all seashores are the same and they each have their own special kinds of wildlife. Rocky shores are the best ones to explore because the rock crevices and seaweeds provide plenty of shelter for animals. There may also be rock pools in which you can see SEA ANEMONES, CRABS, and small FISH. Sandy shores are home to huge numbers of WORMS and MOLLUSKS which burrow under the surface. When the tide comes in, it brings millions of tiny plants and animals with it. These provide food for the mollusks. Large pieces of seaweed are often washed up on the beach, where they are eaten by sandhoppers and other small creatures. They are themselves eaten by CRABS and seabirds. Wading birds, such as oystercatchers, walk over the rocks, or probe into the mud for food. Other seabirds, such as PUFFINS, come to the coast only to breed.

SEASHORES IN DANGER

Oil tankers cause damage to the seashore when they have accidents. Thousands of tons of oil may spill into the sea and onto beaches. The oil poisons seals and seabirds and kills the smaller animals of the shore. It often takes years for wildlife to recover.

LIFE ON A SEASHORE

1 Guillemot
2 Puffin and sand eels
3 Limpet
4 Mussel
5 Goby
6 Barnacle
7 Beadlet anemone
8 Common shrimp
9 Hermit crab
10 Opelet anemone
11 Periwinkle
12 Edible crab
13 Sea urchin (shell)
14 Black-headed gull
15 Oystercatcher
16 Common cockle
17 Razor clam
18 Common starfish
19 Venus shell
20 Prickly cockle
21 Whelk
22 Shore crab
23 Compass jellyfish
24 Brittlestar
25 Moon jellyfish

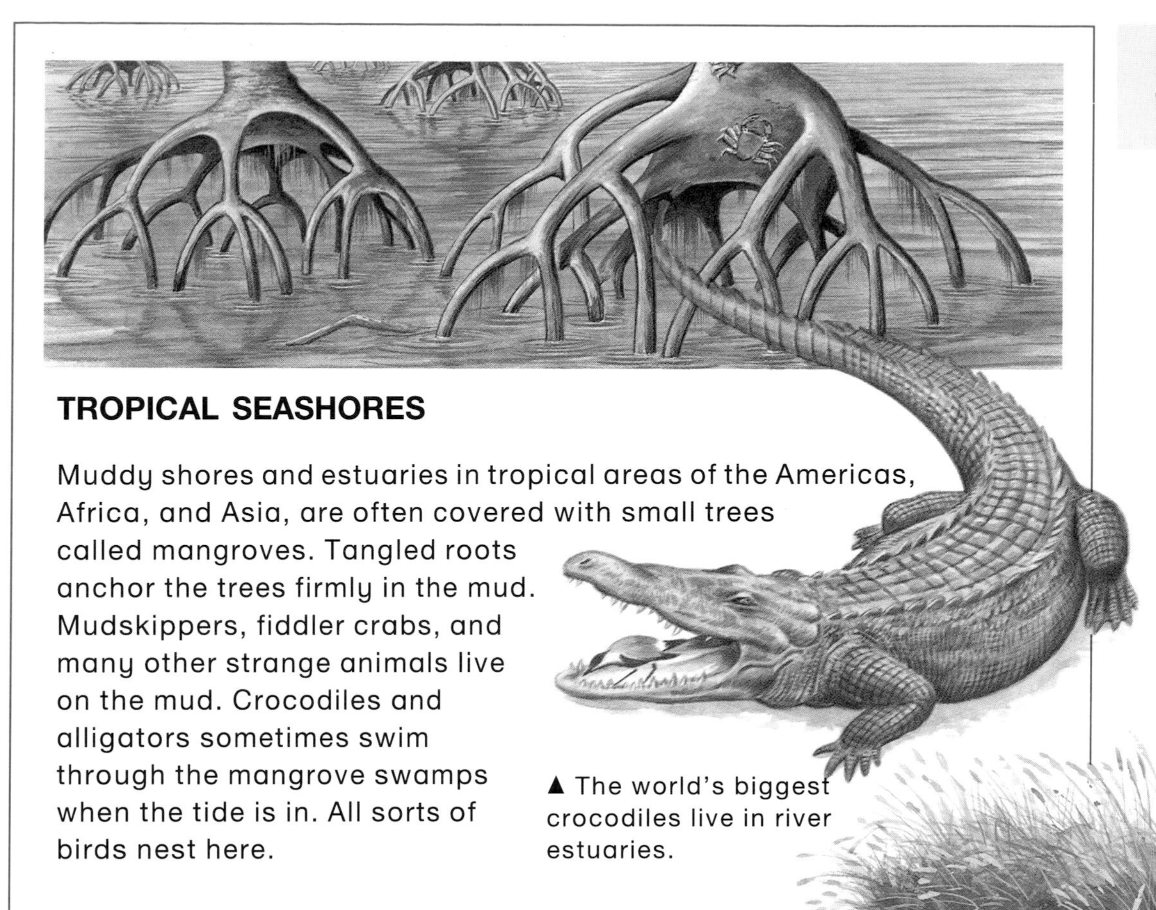

TROPICAL SEASHORES

Muddy shores and estuaries in tropical areas of the Americas, Africa, and Asia, are often covered with small trees called mangroves. Tangled roots anchor the trees firmly in the mud. Mudskippers, fiddler crabs, and many other strange animals live on the mud. Crocodiles and alligators sometimes swim through the mangrove swamps when the tide is in. All sorts of birds nest here.

▲ The world's biggest crocodiles live in river estuaries.

▼ A shark keeps growing new teeth. Whenever a tooth falls out, a new one takes its place.

shark

Sharks have streamlined bodies and unlike most FISH, they have skeletons made of rubbery cartilage instead of bone. Some sharks, such as the dogfish, can be less than 3 feet (1 m) long, but the great white shark, one of the most dangerous species, reaches a length of 20 feet (6 m). See **whale shark**.

shearwater

These medium-sized seagoing BIRDS feed on fish and squid, snatching their food from the surface, or diving after it underwater. Shearwaters nest in burrows on small islands where there are no mammal predators.

▶ Shearwaters usually arrive at their burrows after dark, when there is less risk of being attacked by gulls.

sheep

The farm sheep are descended from a wild RUMINANT known as a mouflon. The mouflon lives in MOUNTAINS in a few parts of southern Europe. There are other species of wild sheep, including the bighorn of the Rocky mountains and the Barbary sheep of North Africa.

shellfish see **mollusks**

shoebill

Also known as the whalehead stork, this strange BIRD has a massive head and a beak shaped like a shoe. It lives in the marshlands of East Africa, and feeds on frogs, fish, water snakes, and shellfish.

▲ Most shrews live in grassy ground, but some are good swimmers and feed underwater.

shrew

The smallest MAMMAL on Earth is a shrew known as the Etruscan pygmy shrew which lives along the coasts of the Mediterranean Sea and the coasts of Africa. It measures only 3 inches (8 cm) from its nose to the tip of the tail. Other shrews are also small and can be recognized by their long pointed noses.

shrike

Shrikes are small BIRDS that pounce on insects, lizards, and mice. They are found in the warmer parts of Europe, Africa, Asia, and North America, and they live in scrub, woodland, and grassland. Shrikes have a habit of "skewering" their food on thorns. They either tear up the skewered food, or store it for the future.

shrimp

Shrimps are small CRUSTACEANS that have a single pair of pincers. Like their relatives the PRAWNS, they are found throughout the world, mainly in salt water. Shrimps prey on worms, young fish, and crustaceans, and also scavenge for food particles.

sidewinder

This nocturnal North American SNAKE lives in desert areas with soft sand and has an unusual way of moving. Instead of zigzagging across the ground, it loops its body through the air, rather like someone taking quick sideways steps.

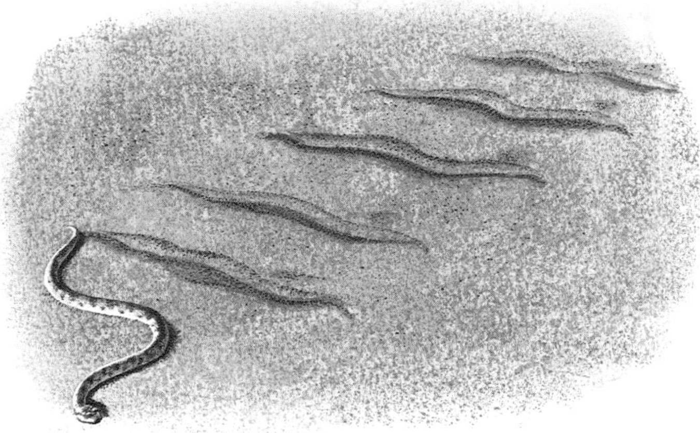

▲ The sidewinder's special kind of movement leaves distinctive tracks in the desert sand.

silkmoth

Many insects and spiders spin silk threads. The silkmoth caterpillar uses silk to make a protective shell, called a coccoon, and inside the coccoon it gradually changes into an adult moth. The caterpillars, or silkworms, are often raised in captivity, and their coccoons are carefully unwound to produce silk for making clothes. Silkworms are reared on mulberry leaves. The wild ancestor of the silkmoth lived in China but silkworms are now raised all over the world.

▲ Skates live on the seabed, and feed on crabs, lobsters, and occasionally octopuses.

skate

This oddly-shaped fish is related to the RAYS. It is found in the Atlantic Ocean and the Mediterranean Sea, and can be as much as 8 feet (2.4 m) across.

skimmer

A skimmer flies low over calm water at dusk, and hunts with the help of its very unusual beak. The beak has a long lower half, and this slices through the surface of the water. If the skimmer touches an animal, its beak snaps shut.

▼ If the skimmer catches a fish, it swallows it while on the move.

skunk

Skunks are small stripy MAMMALS that defend themselves by spraying an evil-smelling liquid. Apart from its nasty smell, the fluid also makes eyes sting and skin itch. Skunks are found in North and South America. See **defense**.

▲ A sloth has tiny green plants growing in its fur.

sloth

There are five different species of sloth, and all of them are found in South and Central America. Sloths feed on leaves and they spend their entire lives hanging from branches by their curved claws.

slowworm

Slowworms look like small SNAKES, but they are actually LIZARDS that have no legs. Slowworms eat slugs, worms, insects, and spiders, and are found in fields, gardens, and heathland throughout most of Europe, and in parts of Asia and Africa.

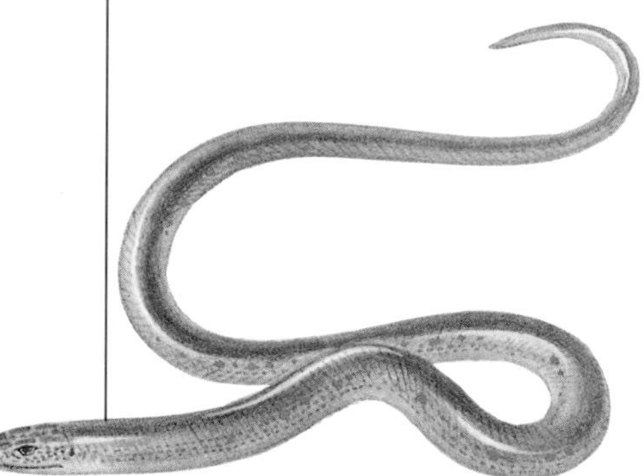

◀ Unlike snakes, a slowworm has eyelids, and tiny holes leading into its ears.

slug

Slugs are relatives of SNAILS that have lost their shells. They have thick leathery skins, and they are covered by a layer of mucus which stops them from drying out. Most slugs feed on plants, but some eat earthworms and even other slugs.

snail

A snail is a MOLLUSK whose soft body is protected by a hard coiled shell. If danger threatens or the weather becomes very dry, the snail pulls itself into its shell. Snails are found throughout the world except in deserts. Some snails live on land and breathe through lungs, while others live in water and breathe through gills. Most land snails eat leaves, flowers, and other parts of plants, while many sea snails are predators.

▶ Snails leave a trail of slime behind them.

snake

Snakes are REPTILES that have evolved from animals similar to LIZARDS. During the course of evolution, they gradually lost their legs. A snake's body is covered with scales, and it has extra-wide scales on its underside to help it grip the ground. Many snakes produce venom to kill their prey, and some snakes inject their venom through hollow teeth called fangs.

snow leopard

Few people have ever seen a snow leopard because these large CATS are extremely rare and very shy of humans. They have a grayish-white coat, with blackish-brown spots similar to those of a LEOPARD. Snow leopards live in the Himalayas and other MOUNTAINS in Pakistan, Afghanistan, and China. They are a little smaller than leopards, reaching a maximum length of 5 feet (1.5 m). Wild sheep and goats make up most of their food, along with large birds such as pheasants and partridges.

S

snowy owl

An inhabitant of the Arctic, the snowy owl has white feathers with black markings. The feathers cover its toes, as protection against the extreme cold. Unlike most owls, snowy owls hunt during the day.

▲ The snowy owl catches lemming, hares, and nesting birds.

sparrow

Several kinds of small brownish bird are known as sparrows. Most sparrows feed on a mixture of seeds and insects. The common house sparrow originally lived only in Europe, Asia, and North Africa.

sparrow hawk

Sparrow hawks are small BIRDS OF PREY. The European sparrow hawk eats sparrows, along with other small birds. The American sparrow hawk is quite different. It is a kind of KESTREL.

sperm whale

Sperm whales are the largest whales that have teeth, and can grow up to 65 feet (20 m) long. They dive to search for squid, and find their prey by sound, using an echolocation system similar to that of BATS. Sperm whales are found throughout the oceans of the world.

▼ The sperm whale can dive to a depth of half a mile, and it can stay underwater for up to an hour.

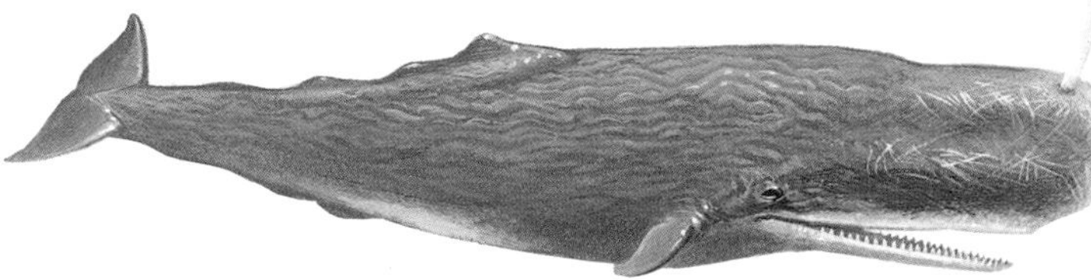

spider

Spiders have eight legs, which makes them easy to distinguish from INSECTS, which have only six. All spiders are predators and most have powerful jaws and a poisonous bite. See **arachnids**.

▶ Some spiders spin webs, but others catch their prey by jumping on it.

spider crab

The largest CRUSTACEAN in the world is a spider crab, found off the shores of Japan. It can span 26 feet (8 m), although most of this distance is made up by its long legs. Other spider crabs are much smaller.

spider monkey

These slender MONKEYS are found in South America. They feed mainly on fruit. Using its long tail, a spider monkey can hang from a branch. See **rain forests**.

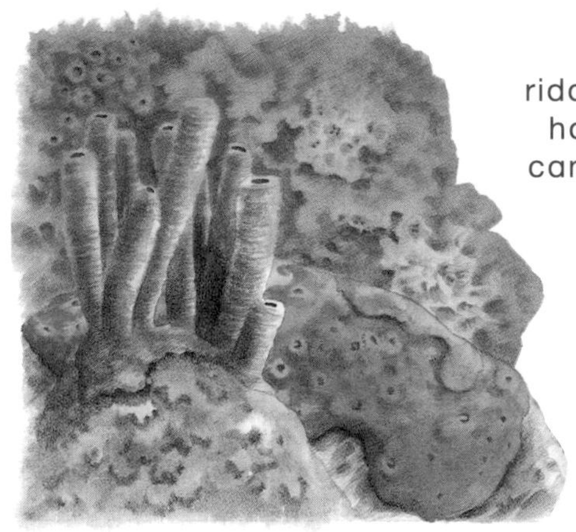

◀ A sponge is riddled with small holes that water can flow through.

sponge
Sponges are among the simplest of all animals. They feed by taking in sea water, filtering out small particles of food, then squirting the water out again.

spoonbill
A spoonbill is a large long-legged water BIRD. It feeds by walking along slowly with its bill partly in the water. It swings it from side to side, and if the bill touches any small animal, it quickly eats it.

◀ Spoonbills live only in places with quite warm climates. One species is found in the Americas, and several others in Europe, Africa, Asia, Australia, and New Zealand.

springbok
Like their close relatives the GAZELLES, springbok leap high into the air if they are alarmed. Springbok live in southern Africa in grassy regions known as veld, and they stay together in small herds.

squid
Squid are MOLLUSKS with holster-shaped bodies and ten tentacles surrounding their mouths. They are related to CUTTLEFISH and OCTOPUSES, and some of them grow to over 50 feet (15 m) long, if their tentacles are included. However, most squid are far smaller than this. They live in huge shoals, feeding on small fish.

▲ Squirrels have good eyesight, and can run through the treetops as fast as a person running along the ground.

squirrel
Except in Australia, squirrels are found almost wherever there are forests. These tree-living RODENTS have sharp claws that grip branches and bushy tails that help them to balance. They are well known for feeding on nuts, but they also eat other food including insects, eggs, and bark. See **ground squirrel**.

stag beetle
The "antlers" of the male stag beetle are used for fighting other males, just like the antlers of deer. These large BEETLES fly at night and feed on drops of sweet sap that ooze from the trunks of trees. Their grubs feed on rotting wood in fallen tree-trunks or old tree stumps.

starfish

Starfish are common ECHINODERMS that usually have five arms. They are found in shallow sea water throughout the world, and all are predators, feeding on mollusks, fish, corals, or other starfish.

▼ The common starling slowly turns black as it grows up.

starling

Starlings are small to medium-sized birds that are black or sometimes brightly colored. They eat a great variety of food, including worms, insects, fruit, and grain, and are very adaptable.

stick insect

A stick insect looks just like a stick. To make the most of its disguise, it can keep perfectly still for long periods. When it moves, it walks very slowly, and even sways just like a twig in the wind. Stick insects are mainly found in tropical areas of the world. See **camouflage**.

▼ The stonefish has poisonous spines on its back. Its venom is powerful enough to kill a human.

stingray

The "sting" of the stingray is in its tail, and is a venomous spike that sticks up at an angle when this FISH lies buried in the seabed. A stingray uses its sting mainly for defense, and its venom is powerful enough to kill anyone who accidentally steps on it. Like other RAYS, stingrays "fly" through the water by flapping the large wing-like fins at the sides of their bodies. They feed on small fish and shellfish.

stoat

Stoats are MAMMALS that are related to WEASELS and MARTENS. They have thin bodies which allow them to run through rabbit burrows to find their prey.

▶ In winter the stoat's fur turns white in northern regions. It is then called ermine.

stonefish

Found in the Indian Ocean and the Pacific, these small knobbly-bodied FISH are among the most poisonous in the world. Stonefish lie half-buried on the seabed in shallow water, and are well camouflaged. Stonefish use their CAMOUFLAGE to ambush small fish and other animals.

▲ Storks often nest on houses. People encourage them because they are thought to bring good luck.

stork

Storks are long-legged BIRDS that snap up insects and other small animals with their large bills. They are found throughout the warmer parts of the world.

sturgeon

These FISH are famous because their eggs are sold as "caviar," which is one of the most expensive foods in the world. Sturgeons can grow up to 10 feet (3 m) long, and are found only in cold FRESH-WATER in the Northern Hemisphere.

▲ Sturgeons feed on worms, mussels, and other small animals.

swallow

Swooping through the air, swallows catch flies and other insects on the wing. In places with cool climates, swallows are summer visitors, and after breeding they migrate to warmer places. They are found in all parts of the world. Many kinds of swallow have forked tails. Swallows often nest in open buildings. See **migration**.

swallowtail

A swallowtail is a large and spectacular BUTTERFLY with "tails" on its hindwings. The two tails make a shape like a SWALLOW's tail, and this is how these butterflies got their name. Swallowtails live mainly in warm places.

▶ Swallowtails are good fliers. They often live for a long time compared to many butterflies.

swan

A graceful creature when swimming, the swan is slow and clumsy on land. These large BIRDS are found around lakes, large rivers, and coastal areas. They eat waterplants, together with crustaceans and other small animals found in the water.

▼ A swan's young are called cygnets.

swift

Swifts are among the best fliers of all BIRDS, and often spend weeks or even months on the wing. They have long crescent-shaped wings, but small weak legs, and they cannot walk or perch. Swifts eat insects, and they catch their prey in mid-air, as SWALLOWS do. During the day they often swoop low over fields and buildings, but at night they climb high into the sky and sleep on the wing. Swifts migrate to breed, and most parts of the world, except New Zealand and the southern part of South America, see swifts at some time of the year. See **migration**.

▼ The swordfish's long upper jaw is a lethal weapon similar to that of the marlin.

swordfish

The long swordlike jaw of the swordfish is one of the mysteries of the animal kingdom: no one knows exactly what it is for. The swords are sometimes found embedded in whales, and have occasionally pierced wooden boats, although probably not deliberately. Swordfish can swim at speeds of 60 miles (100 km) an hour, making it hard for them to stop suddenly. They may use their swords to stun fish, swimming through schools while shaking their heads.

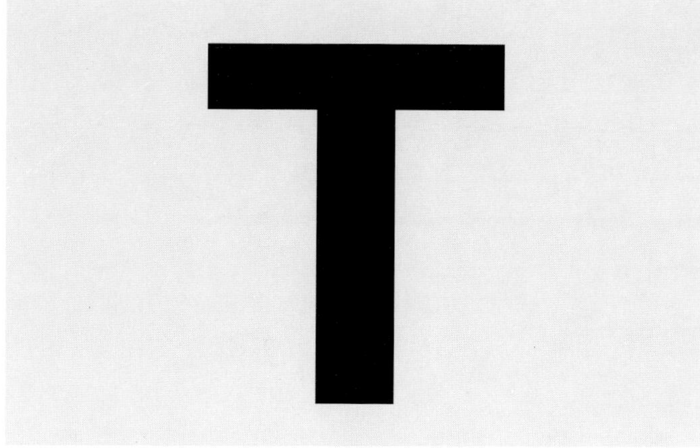

tanager

Few BIRDS are as colorful as the tanagers, with their brilliant patches of green, yellow, blue, and red, or red and black, or brown and pink. These small birds are found only in the American tropics and subtropics, although some migrate into cooler areas of North America in the summer. They feed on fruit or nectar.

tapir

The black-and-white Malayan tapir is a small leaf-eating MAMMAL related to HORSES. It lives in the tropical forests of Southeast Asia. It has a long nose, which it uses like a trunk. The Brazilian tapir is similar, but is brown all over.

▼ A tapir's nose is long and flexible, and it uses it to pull leaves toward its mouth.

tarantula

The name tarantula is often used for large hairy SPIDERS found in the forests of South America. They eat prey such as small lizards, frogs, snakes, and birds. The proper name for these is "BIRD-EATING SPIDERS." True tarantulas are actually small but venomous spiders found in Europe. See **trapdoor spider**.

▲ Tarantulas often lie in wait for their prey hiding in burrows.

tarsier

The tarsier lives in the forests of Malaysia, Indonesia, and the Philippines. It is one of the smallest PRIMATES and, when fully grown, its body measures only 4–6 inches (10–15 cm) long. Tarsiers are nocturnal. They feed mainly on insects but they sometimes catch young birds.

Tasmanian devil

Found only in Tasmania, this MARSUPIAL mammal is the size of a small dog and is very fierce. Like a HYENA, it has an unusually large head and powerful jaws for cracking open bones.

▼ Tasmanian devils eat wild animals and also scavenge food from dead sheep on farms.

termite

Like other social INSECTS, termites live in huge family groups, called colonies, and they build special nests. A termite nest is often a high mound built from soil mixed with termite saliva and droppings. Inside the nest only one female, called the queen, lays eggs. Some of her young become worker termites that collect food, while others become soldiers that defend the nest. Termites are mainly found in warm parts of the world.

▶ A tern hovers over the sea.

tern

Terns are small seabirds, related to SEAGULLS. They have narrow pointed wings. Terns are found on coasts around the world, and some of them migrate long distances. One species, the Arctic tern, travels almost from pole to pole—farther than other bird. See **migration**.

terrapin

These small TURTLES live on the coasts of North America, in saltmarshes and mudflats. They feed on INVERTEBRATES such as worms, clams, and water snails during the day, burying themselves in the mud at night. Terrapins grow to about 10 inches (25 cm) in length, and sometimes have brightly striped skin.

thrush

Most thrushes are medium-sized dark BIRDS with speckled or colored breasts. They feed on insects, earthworms, berries, and other fruit, and are found in woodland, farmland, and gardens. Thrushes live in most parts of the world.

▼ Tigers usually live alone. Males and females meet only to breed.

tiger

Larger than a LION or LEOPARD, the tiger is the biggest and most powerful member of the CAT family. It can reach 9 feet (2.8 m) in length, with its tail adding nearly another yard. Tigers live in a wide range of wooded habitats, from the hot plains of India to Siberia. Unlike lions, they hunt mainly at night. Tigers eat deer, bison, buffalo and wild pigs, but if they are injured they may also attack humans.

tit

Tits, or titmice, are small neat birds with short beaks that are common in woodland, scrub, and yards. They hunt for aphids and other insects, and often hang upside down while they are feeding. Tits live throughout most of the Northern Hemisphere.

▲ Some toads have bright colors to warn that their skin is poisonous.

toad

There is no sharp dividing line between toads and FROGS, but the word "toad" is normally used for heavily-built AMPHIBIANS that have dry, warty skins and that move by walking instead of hopping. Toads are found throughout the world, except in polar regions.

tortoise

Tortoises are among the most ancient REPTILES on Earth. A tortoise's heavy shell makes it slow and clumsy, but also gives it plenty of protection from predators. Tortoises live mainly in warm parts of Europe, Asia, Africa, and North America.

toucan

The toucan uses its huge and colorful beak to reach fruit in its forest home. It is probably used in displays as well, in the breeding season. As well as eating fruit, toucans also eat birds' eggs, nestlings, and small reptiles. There are 37 species of these birds, and they are found only in South America.

▶ A toucan's beak looks heavy, but it is filled with air spaces.

T

trapdoor spider

Trapdoor spiders make underground burrows that have a hinged lid made of silk. At night they open the lid just slightly, and wait for small animals to come their way. As soon as something steps on the trapdoor, the spider grabs it, and drags it inside.

▲ A trapdoor spider attacks when it senses a passing insect.

tree frog

In the RAIN FORESTS many FROGS live their whole lives above ground. These tree frogs are all very small and light. They have large toes with ridged pads that cling to leaves. Like other frogs, they eat insects.

tree shrew

Tree shrews are small MAMMALS that live in the forests of Southeast Asia. They have long pointed noses and long tails, which are sometimes bushy. They live mainly on insects and also on fruit. See **primate**.

▲ Trout are often raised in fish farms.

trout

Close relatives of the SALMON, trout are smaller FISH that often have pretty and intricate markings. Some kinds of trout spend all their lives in rivers or lakes, but others migrate to the sea, and return to rivers to breed. Originally trout were found only in the Northern Hemisphere. They feed on small animals such as insects and crustaceans, or on fish.

tsetse fly

Without the tsetse fly, there would be far more farms in Africa and far fewer wild animals. This is because this tropical FLY spreads sleeping sickness, a serious disease that affects both people and cattle. The fly feeds on blood by making a small cut in the skin, and as it laps up its meal the infection passes into the blood. Wild animals are not badly affected by the disease. For cattle, horses, and humans, the disease can be fatal.

▲ Sharks are among the tuna's few natural enemies.

tuna

Tuna are large and powerful ocean-going FISH that prefer to live in warmer waters. They tend to swim in large schools, pursuing smaller fish, squid, and some crustaceans like hunters in a pack. Tuna are fast swimmers and are found throughout the tropics. Large numbers of tuna are caught every year by people.

tundra see **pages 130 and 131**

▶ Domesticated turkeys are raised for their meat in many parts of the world.

turkey

Despite their name, wild turkeys come from North and South America. They were domesticated by the Mexican Indians and are now raised for their meat in many parts of the world. Wild turkeys live in open forests, searching for seeds, berries, and insects on the forest floor by day, and roosting in the trees at night.

▶ The green turtle returns to the same beach year after year to lay its eggs.

turtle

Turtles are REPTILES that are closely related to TORTOISES. They all live in water. Freshwater turtles lay their eggs in mud by the shore, or hidden under logs or dead leaves. Ocean-going turtles have to come ashore to lay, and they lumber up beaches on dark nights before dropping their eggs into a pit in the sand. The world's largest turtle is the leatherback, which can weigh half a ton. This enormous animal has a soft shell, and lives mainly on jellyfish.

▲ Lots of animals are ungulates, including horses.

ungulates

An ungulate is any MAMMAL that has hooves. Hooves are made of a hard material, keratin, which also makes up skin, hair, and fingernails. They are useful for animals that run fast, such as HORSES, ANTELOPE, and DEER, and they provide good grip for mountain animals such as GOATS, wild SHEEP, and CHAMOIS. Some ungulates have just a single hoof in contact with the ground, while others have two. The hooves of the chamois have a spongy inner pad surrounded by a hard outer rim which helps to stop it slipping on smooth rock or icy surfaces.

T

TUNDRA

In the far north, large areas are so cold that trees cannot grow. Beneath the surface the soil is often frozen solid, and the ground is covered with pools and lakes that cannot drain away. This is tundra, one of the most remote and inhospitable habitats on Earth. For most of the year the tundra is cold and still, but in spring and summer there is a sudden explosion of life. Midges and mosquitoes breed in the pools in huge numbers, and the insects and plants provide food for visiting birds. Predators such as ARCTIC FOXES and SNOWY OWLS prey on the birds and their nestlings, and also on VOLES, LEMMINGS, and ARCTIC HARES which live on the tundra plants. Herds of REINDEER often move northward into the tundra to feed during the summer, and during the fall the POLAR BEAR, a visitor from the Arctic, arrives to feed on berries.

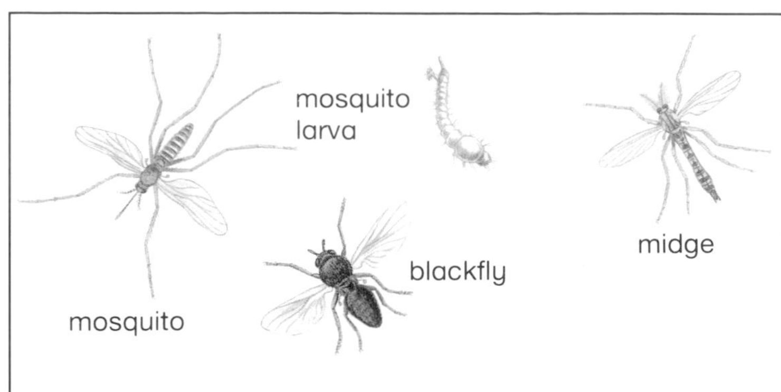

INSECTS OF THE TUNDRA

Tundra is full of bogs and pools, and these are perfect breeding places for mosquitoes, midges, and other biting insects. These insects spend the winter as eggs. The eggs hatch in spring. In summer adults take to the air.

TUNDRA LIFE

1 Musk ox
2 Snow bunting
3 Ptarmigan
4 Dunlin
5 Arctic hare
6 Pectoral sandpiper
7 Snow goose
8 Gray plover
9 Arctic tern
10 Reindeer
11 Arctic fox
12 Lemming
13 Snowy owl
14 Clouded yellow butterfly

WINTER IN THE TUNDRA

Some animals stay in the tundra when the snow and ice returns. Some of these animals turn white, which makes them difficult to see against the snow. When the summer comes again they turn brown so that they still blend in with their background.

arctic hare
northern gray wolf
arctic fox
ermine
ptarmigan

TUNDRA IN DANGER

At one time, people survived in the tundra by hunting and fishing, or by herding reindeer. Today, the tundra is also the home of engineers drilling for oil. The remote tundra is being opened up, increasing the danger of pollution and threatening tundra animals.

▼ During the summer, the Sun never sets over the tundra, so it is light for 24 hours a day. Once the surface has thawed, tundra plants grow very quickly, and for a few weeks, there is lots of food. Herds of reindeer migrate north into the tundra to make use of this food. The snowy owl preys on plant-feeding rodents, such as lemmings. Unlike most owls, it has to attack in broad daylight.

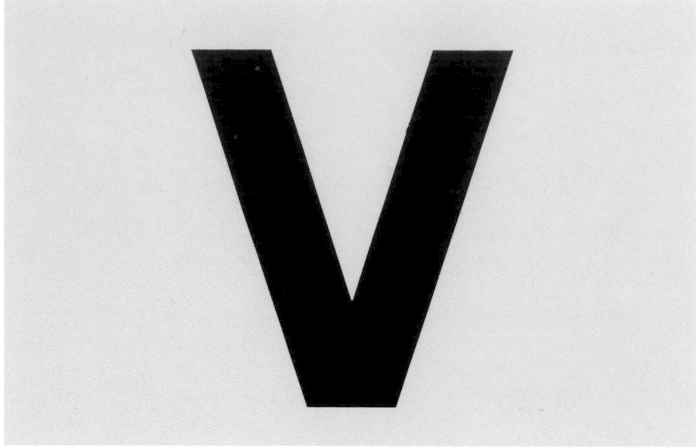

vampire bat

Alone among the MAMMALS, the vampire bat lives by drinking blood. Vampire bats take blood from any large animal, including cattle, horses, and people. They feed on moonless nights and probably detect their victims by smell. A vampire bat lands nearby and then scuttles over to its victim. With two sharp front teeth it cuts the skin to make the blood flow, and it then laps up the blood with its tongue.

VERTEBRATES

Most vertebrates have keen senses and quick reactions. Vertebrates are found all over the world in all kinds of habitat, from high mountains to the depths of the sea.

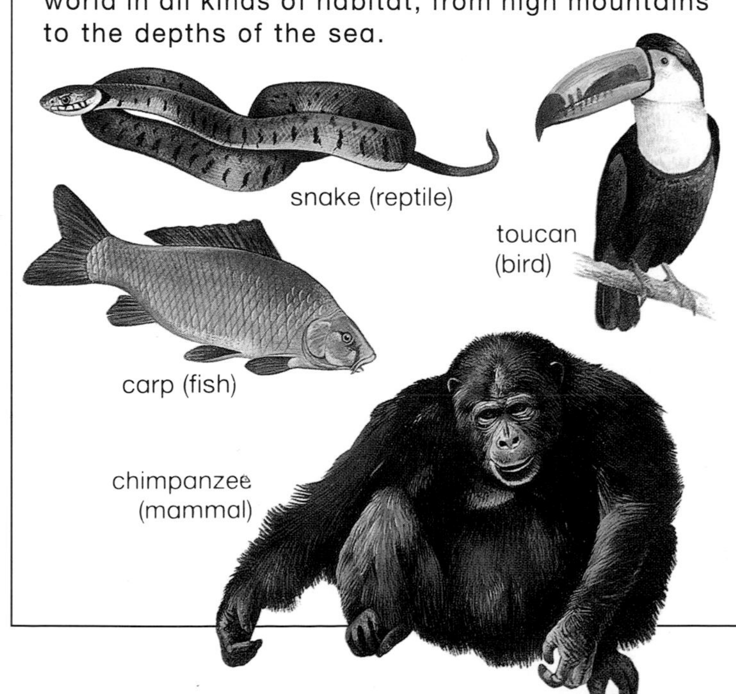

vertebrates

The vertebrates first appeared on Earth over 400 million years ago. This large group of animals includes all the FISH, AMPHIBIANS, REPTILES, BIRDS, and MAMMALS. Vertebrates all have a long backbone running through the body, and this is made up of bones called vertebrae. See **invertebrates**.

◀ Vicuñas are large grass-eating mammals.

vicuña

Vicuñas live high in the Andes mountains of South America. Vicuñas were once at risk of extinction due to overhunting but are now increasing in numbers.

vole

Voles are RODENTS that are closely related to the LEMMINGS. Unlike a MOUSE, they have short and rather fat bodies, and a blunt rounded nose. They feed on plants.

vulture

Vultures are large scavenging BIRDS. They generally live in open grasslands, MOUNTAINS, and DESERTS, and they spend the day soaring high over the ground. Vultures have very keen eyesight, and if one vulture spots a meal, others follow it from far around. Most vultures have long bare necks, and this helps them to reach inside a carcass. See **condor**.

wallaby
Apart from their smaller size, there is no real difference between wallabies and KANGAROOS. Together, they form a group of plant-eating MARSUPIAL mammals found only in Australia and New Guinea.

walrus
Two very long curved tusks make this large sea MAMMAL unmistakable. A male walrus's tusks can be over 3 feet (1 m) long, while the female's are much smaller. Walruses live around the Arctic and they dive to feed on clams and other shellfish on the muddy seabed. No one knows for certain how they get at their food, but they probably dig animals out with their tusks, and then scoop them up in their large bristly mouths. Walruses are related to SEALS and SEALIONS, and large males can weigh up to one and a half tons.

▼ A walrus's tusks are made of ivory, like the tusks of an elephant.

wapiti see **red deer**

warbler
Warblers are small shy BIRDS that search for caterpillars, spiders, and similar prey among the leaves of trees and bushes. They usually have rather dull colors, and the best way to identify a warbler is often by its song. Warblers are found in woodlands, gardens, marshes, and a variety of other HABITATS. One group of warblers inhabits Europe, Asia, Africa, and Australia, while a different group is found in the Americas. Many warblers migrate to raise their young.

▼ Warblers have sharp, narrow beaks for picking up small insects.

warthog
Few animals are quite as ugly as the warthog. This African MAMMAL is a type of wild PIG, and it lives in grasslands and woodlands. Warthogs have curved tusks and lumps on their faces, and this gives them their name. Like other pigs, warthogs eat a wide range of food. In the dry season they dig up plant roots, and at other times of the year they eat grass, fruit, and dead animals.

▼ Wasps make their nests either out of mud, or out of chewed-up wood.

wasp

The bright yellow and black stripes of these common INSECTS act as a warning, showing that wasps are dangerous and should not be touched. They have very slender "waists," and many of them live in family groups and build nests. Wasps are found throughout the world. See **hornet**.

water spider

Spiders cannot breathe under water, but water spiders still manage to live below the surface. They store air in special silk "diving bells" attached to underwater plants. These provide the spider with oxygen, so that it can hunt underwater.

▶ A waxwing has a large crest on its head, making it easy to recognize.

waxwing

These medium-sized gray-brown BIRDS get their name from the row of red "beads" on each wing, which look like drops of wax. Waxwings eat berries and other fruit, and live in forests and gardens in much of the Northern Hemisphere.

weasel

The weasel is the smallest predatory MAMMAL. Although its body is about 8 inches (20 cm) long, it is so slender that it can easily fit into a mouse's burrow. Weasels live mainly on mice and voles, and they usually hunt after dark. They have a bouncing, looping way of running, and they often sit up on their back legs to get a better view of their surroundings. Weasels live throughout Europe and North America. See **stoat**.

▼ A weasel's front and back legs are far apart, and its body is not much thicker than an adult's finger.

weaverbird

Weaverbirds are among the finest nest-builders in the animal world. These small brown or yellow BIRDS nest in trees, and they build their nests by weaving grass to make a hollow ball. Most weaverbirds feed mainly on seeds, and they live in the GRASSY PLAINS of Africa.

weevil

These small BEETLES nearly all live on plants, and they have long snouts that are sometimes as long as the rest of the body. Weevils often bore their way through their food, and they can cause a tremendous amount of damage to crops. Weevils are found in most parts of the world.

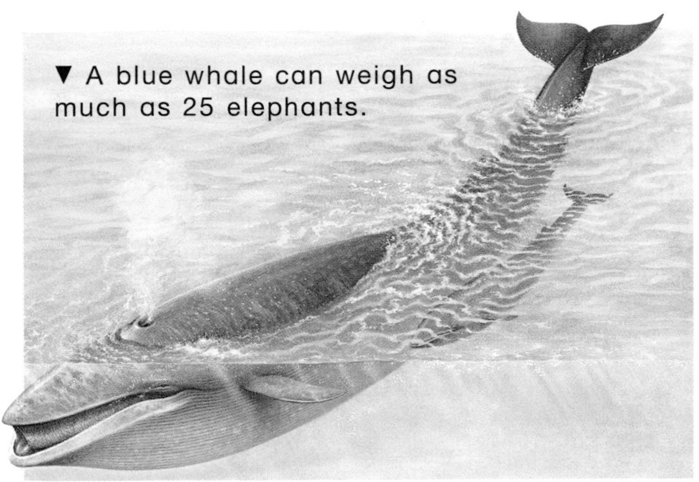

▼ A blue whale can weigh as much as 25 elephants.

whale

Whales are sea-living MAMMALS. They are found throughout the oceans and are highly adapted for a life at sea. Some whales hunt other animals, but the biggest whales of all, the BLUE WHALES, sieve tiny animals from the water using long fringed plates in their mouths.

whalehead stork see **shoebill**

whale shark

The gigantic whale shark reaches over 50 feet (15 m) in length, and looks extremely dangerous. But despite being the biggest FISH on Earth, it is harmless to humans. Like the BLUE WHALE, another giant of the seas, it feeds by filtering tiny animals from the water. The whale shark is found throughout the tropical seas, although it is not very common.

▼ The whale shark filters its food out of the water by using its gills as sieves.

wildebeest see **gnu**

winkle

Winkles are small seashore MOLLUSKS that are closely related to SNAILS. Like snails, they have coiled shells and muscular bodies, and they can pull their bodies into their shells when danger threatens. Winkles feed by scraping tiny plants from the rocks. See **seashore**.

▲ Despite their bad reputation, wolves do not attack people.

wolf

The gray or timber wolf is the ancestor of our pet dogs. Today wolves survive only in the wildest areas, such as the forests of northern Canada and Siberia. They live in packs, and they tackle large animals by working together as a team.

wombat

Like other MARSUPIALS, wombats have a pouch. But instead of pointing forward, the wombat's pouch opens near the animal's rear end. Wombats are heavy-bodied animals, and can be over 3 feet (1 m) long. They are found in forests mainly in the southeast of Australia.

wood louse

The only CRUSTACEANS to have made a home for themselves on land, wood lice are remarkably successful and are found all over the world. They feed on waste matter and decaying plant material, including wood. When threatened, some wood lice can roll up into a ball, so that their softer undersides are protected by their armored body plates.

▲ Most woodpeckers eat insect grubs. The green woodpecker eats ants on the ground, and the acorn woodpecker collects acorns and stores them in holes that it makes.

woodpecker

Woodpeckers do not eat wood, but the grubs of wood-boring insects which live deep inside tree trunks. A woodpecker drills a hole into the trunk by hammering with its beak, and then feels for insects with its very long tongue, which has a spiky tip. Woodpeckers live in wooded places throughout the world, except in Australia, Madagascar, and many small islands. See **coniferous forests, deciduous forests**.

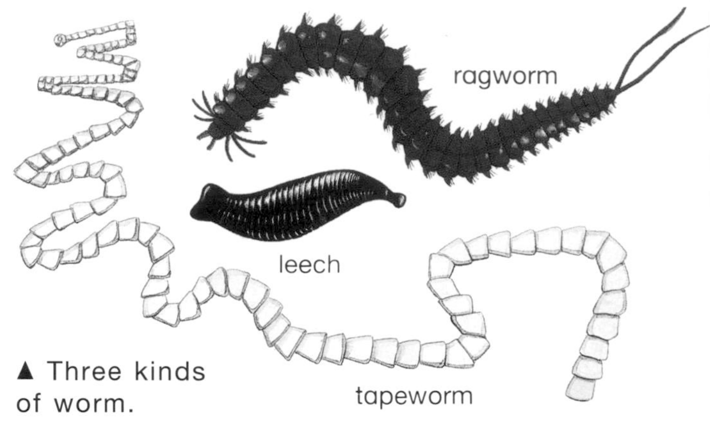

▲ Three kinds of worm.

worms

Many different kinds of animal are called worms. The ones that most people know are EARTHWORMS that live in soil all over the world. Like LEECHES and lugworms, an earthworm's body is divided into segments, and it belongs to a group of worms called the annelids. Most other worms are simpler, and do not have segments. Some live in plants or in the soil, but others are PARASITES that live inside other animals. Roundworms often live in plants or animals. Tapeworms live in the intestines of various animals, including humans.

▶ The Carolina wren is just one of many American wren species.

wren

Wrens are small or tiny brown insect-eating BIRDS that live mainly in the Americas, although one species is found throughout Europe, and parts of Africa and Asia. Wrens have short, upright tails and despite their small size, very loud songs. They mainly live in farmland, woodland, gardens, and parks.

◀ Yaks are kept for their milk, and used for carrying loads.

yak

High up in the Himalayas, the climate is too harsh for many animals. But the yak, a hardy MAMMAL with a long shaggy coat, is well adapted to these difficult conditions. See **buffalo**, **ruminants**.

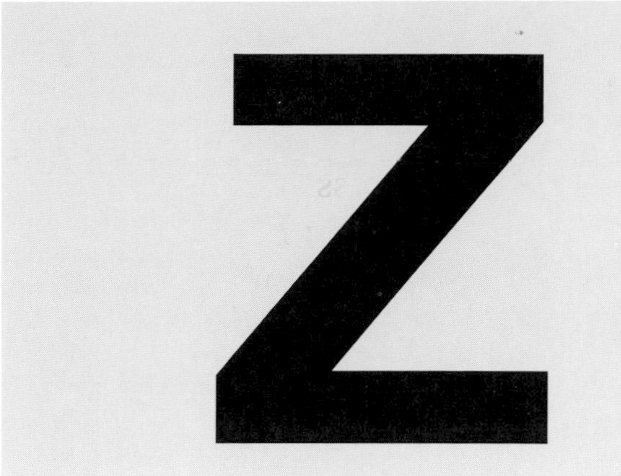

zebra

Zebras are stripy grass-eating MAMMALS found in eastern and southern Africa. They are closely related to HORSES, and they rely on keen senses and speed to escape their enemies. No one knows exactly why zebras have such bright black and white stripes. They might be a form of CAMOUFLAGE, to break up the zebra's outline, or they may be a signal to other zebras, keeping the herd together.

▼ Each zebra has a slightly different pattern of stripes.

Index

Page numbers in *italics* refer to illustrations